William John Hardy

The Handwritings of the Kings and Queens of England

With photogravures and facsims. of signatures and historical documents

William John Hardy

The Handwritings of the Kings and Queens of England
With photogravures and facsims. of signatures and historical documents

ISBN/EAN: 9783337322786

Printed in Europe, USA, Canada, Australia, Japan

Cover: Foto ©ninafisch / pixelio.de

More available books at **www.hansebooks.com**

The Handwriting

of the

Kings & Queens of England

BY

W. J. HARDY, F.S.A.
AUTHOR OF 'BOOK PLATES,' ETC.

*WITH PHOTOGRAVURES AND FACSIMILES OF SIGNATURES
AND HISTORICAL DOCUMENTS*

THE RELIGIOUS TRACT SOCIETY
56 PATERNOSTER ROW AND 65 ST. PAUL'S CHURCHYARD
1893

PREFACE

THE greater part of this work appeared in the pages of the *Leisure Hour* during the years 1889 and 1891, but some of the most interesting examples of royal penmanship, here figured, have not before been made public: indeed, their existence was unknown until recently, when they were discovered, amongst some uncalendared documents at the Public Record Office, by Mr. H. C. Maxwell Lyte, C. B., the present Deputy-Keeper of the Records, by whose kindness, in pointing them out to me, and in giving me permission to have photographs taken of them, I am enabled to include them here.

These new discoveries include some words written by Richard II; a letter wholly in the handwriting of Henry IV; a curious form of the signature of Henry VI, which shows that he used a wood-block stamp with his name upon it; and a long sentence penned by Edward IV— of whose writing no example, except the ordinary 'E. R.,' was known to exist.

The additional examples of royal handwriting that I have given in this volume, also include several documents illustrative of what I may term the religious history of England—part of the draft of 'the Bishops' Book,' showing alterations in the handwriting of Henry VIII; a group of signatures of men intimately connected with the translation of the Bible; a letter from Edward VI to the Senate of Zurich; another letter from the same king, and his Council, to the English Bishops, enjoining the

Preface

use of the English Book of Common Prayer; a letter from Queen Mary to the Justices of Devonshire, thanking the people of that county for their adherence to Roman Catholicism; a letter from Queen Elizabeth to the Dutch Reformed Congregation at Austin Friars; and the draft, corrected by James I, of his letter to the Bishops, which was, in reality, a 'Declaration of Faith.'

To Mr. Maxwell Lyte, and the various officials of the Public Record Office, especially to Mr. Scargill-Bird and Mr. G. H. Overend, I must tender my warmest thanks for continual assistance in collecting materials for the production of this work, and for their readiness in according the permission to take photographs of the documents. I am also much indebted to Mr. E. Maunde Thompson, C.B., the Chief Librarian of the British Museum, as well as to Mr. Scott and Mr. Bickley of that department, for valuable advice and assistance, in collecting materials, and for facilities given in obtaining photographs of the letters, or other examples of handwriting selected. Last, but certainly not least, I must thank the Rev. R. Lovett for his constant advice and assistance in preparing this volume.

W. J. HARDY.

CONTENTS

		PAGE
I.	INTRODUCTION	9
II.	EDWARD THE 'BLACK PRINCE'	11
III.	RICHARD II	13
IV.	HENRY IV	16
V.	HENRY V	19
VI.	HENRY VI	30
VII.	EDWARD IV AND HIS QUEEN, ELIZABETH WYDEVILE	35
VIII.	EDWARD V	41
IX.	RICHARD III	45
X.	HENRY VII	49
XI.	HENRY VIII AND HIS WIVES	52
XII.	EDWARD VI	70
XIII.	'JANE THE QUEEN' AND PHILIP AND MARY	81
XIV.	ELIZABETH	91
XV.	JAMES I AND ANNE OF DENMARK	102
XVI.	CHARLES I AND HENRIETTA MARIA, HENRY PRINCE OF WALES, AND ELIZABETH QUEEN OF BOHEMIA	111
XVII.	OLIVER AND RICHARD CROMWELL	124
XVIII.	CHARLES II AND CATHERINE OF BRAGANZA	129

Contents

		PAGE
XIX.	JAMES II, ANNE HYDE, MARY OF MODENA, AND THE LATER STUARTS	132
XX.	WILLIAM III AND MARY .	140
XXI.	ANNE AND GEORGE OF DENMARK	147
XXII.	GEORGE I .	148
XXIII.	GEORGE II AND WILHELMINA CAROLINA, HIS WIFE	151
XXIV.	GEORGE III AND QUEEN CHARLOTTE	159
XXV.	GEORGE IV, QUEEN CAROLINE, AND THE PRINCESS CHARLOTTE .	164
XXVI.	WILLIAM IV AND QUEEN ADELAIDE	171
XXVII.	VICTORIA .	175

LIST OF ILLUSTRATIONS

LIST OF PHOTOGRAVURE PLATES

Letter from Henry IV. Last seven lines written by the king . . . . Frontispiece.
Form of signatures of Richard II . . . . "
Signature of Henry VI . . . . "
Handwriting of Henry VI. The word 'Henry' is stamped . . . . . "
Letter from Edward IV. The 'RE' at the head and last four lines written by
 the king . . . . to face p. 36
Letter from Edward VI signed by the king at the end . . . . . . " 73
Letter from Queen Elizabeth signed at the head . . . . " 96

LIST OF FACSIMILES

	PAGE		PAGE
Autograph 'motto' of the Black Prince	11	Two forms of Henry VII's signature . .	51
Grant signed by Richard II . . .	14	Letter of Henry VIII to Cardinal Wolsey .	53
Signature (French) of Richard II . .	15	Portion of a document—'the Bishops' Book'	
Letter of Henry IV while Earl of Derby	17	—of the period of the Reformation, con-	
Signature of Henry IV	18	taining alterations in the handwriting of	
Specimens of Henry V's handwriting .	21	Henry VIII	57
Letter of Henry V written in 1419 .	26	Signature of Queen Catherine of Aragon .	60
Handwriting of Henry V in 1421 . .	28	Examples of penmanship of men connected	
Signatures of Humphrey Duke of Glouces-		with the early translation of the Bible.—	
ter, Henry V's brother, Cardinal Beau-		Signatures of Tindale, Latimer, Cran-	
fort, and Jacquetta, wife of the Duke of		mer, Coverdale, Grafton, Vaughan, and	
Bedford	29	Cromwell	61
Signature of Henry VI	31	Handwriting of Anne Boleyn . . .	63
" Henry VI	33	Signature of Jane Seymour	65
" Henry VI preserved at Eton .	34	" Catherine Parr . . .	66
" Edward IV as Duke of York .	35	Stamp used by Henry VIII in the early	
" Edward IV and his brothers,		part of his reign	66
the Dukes of Clarence and Gloucester .	37	Stamp on Henry VIII's Will . . .	66
Receipt in the hand of Elizabeth Wydevile,		Handwriting of Anne of Cleves . .	67
Queen of Edward IV	39	" Edward VI . . .	71
Two signatures of Edward V. . . .	41	Letter from Prince Edward to his mother .	72
Handwriting of Edward V	42	Letter from Edward VI and the Council to	
" Richard III, written in 1483	44	the Bishops	76-77
" Richard III	48	Signature of the Protector Somerset .	79
" Henry VII	48	Handwriting of the Protector Somerset .	80
Signature of Henry VII	50	" Queen Mary	82
Margaret Beaufort's handwriting . .	50	" Lady Jane Grey . .	83

List of Illustrations

	PAGE
Handwriting of Lady Jane Grey	85
Letter to County Justices showing Queen Mary's signature at the head	87
Signatures of Queen Mary and Philip of Spain	89
Two signatures of Queen Mary	90
Handwriting of Queen Elizabeth	92
Letter from Queen Elizabeth to Catherine Parr	93
Two signatures of Queen Elizabeth	97
Endorsement of letter from the Earl of Leicester by Queen Elizabeth	98
Prayer composed by Queen Elizabeth	100
Draft of a letter to the Bishops corrected by James I	104
Handwriting of James I	106
Letter of James I to his son, Charles, Prince of Wales	107
Handwriting of Anne of Denmark	109
„ Charles I	111
Latin letter written by Charles to his brother Henry	113
Signature of Prince Henry	115
„ Princess Elizabeth	115
Handwriting of King Charles	116
Portion of prayer written by Charles I	118
Draft of letter to Queen Henrietta Maria	118
Letter from Queen Henrietta Maria to her Son	122
Letter from Oliver Cromwell to his Wife	125
Signature of Oliver Cromwell	127
„ Richard Cromwell	128
„ Catherine of Braganza	131
Portion of letter from Charles II to Sir George Downing	131
Letter of James II to the Prince of Orange	134-5
Signature of James II	137
„ Anne Hyde	137
Letter from Mary of Modena to Lord Caryll	138
Signature of the 'Old Pretender'	139
„ 'Young Pretender'	139
„ Henry of York	139
Handwriting of William III	140
Letter from Queen Mary to Lady Scarborough, 1692	142
Signature of William III	143
Letter from Queen Anne to the Earl of Nottingham	146
Signature of George, Prince of Denmark	147

	PAGE
Letter from George I to the Emperor Charles V	149
Signature of Queen Caroline of Anspach	152
Letter from George II to the Duke of Newcastle	153
Handwriting of Frederick Prince of Wales	155
Signature of Princess Augusta	156
„ the Duke of Cumberland	156
„ Princess Elizabeth	156
„ Princess Anne	156
„ Princess Mary	156
„ Princess Louisa	156
Letter written by George III to his grandfather when eleven years of age	158
Handwriting of George III	160
Signature of the Duke of York	162
„ the Duke of Cumberland	162
„ the Duke of Cambridge	162
„ Princess Charlotte	162
„ Princess Amelia	162
„ Princess Augusta Sophia	162
„ Princess Elizabeth	162
„ Princess Mary	162
„ George III when insane	163
„ Queen Charlotte	163
Translation from Cicero by George IV when fifteen years of age	165
Signature of George IV as Prince Regent	166
„ George IV as attached to the Coronation Oath	166
Handwriting of Queen Caroline	167
„ Princess Charlotte	168
Letter of William IV to Lady Nelson	170
Signature of William IV	172
„ Queen Adelaide	172
Letter from Queen Victoria to the Women of Great Britain and Ireland	174
Earliest handwriting of Queen Victoria	175
Signature of Queen Victoria to the Coronation Oath	175
Signature of the Prince Consort	176
„ Duke of Kent	176
„ Duchess of Kent	176
„ Prince of Wales	176
„ Princess of Wales	176
„ Duke of Clarence and Avondale	176
„ Duke of York	176
„ Duke of Edinburgh	176
„ Duke of Connaught	176
„ Duke of Albany	176

THE HANDWRITING OF THE KINGS AND QUEENS OF ENGLAND

I

INTRODUCTION

HISTORIANS who have described King John as 'signing and sealing' Magna Charta are responsible for the picture which finds its way into the majority of illustrated English Histories of King John, with evident disinclination depicted on his countenance, scrawling his name with a quill-pen of regal length at the foot of a long strip of parchment which lies on the table before him. No doubt the illustration makes a vivid impression on the minds of most youthful students, and so a certain shock to the feelings is caused when we find out (as we very soon do find out if we give any attention to the history of royal handwriting) that King John did not—and, what is more, probably could not—write either 'Johannes Rex,' or indeed anything else, at the foot of the charter of liberties. The words with which that famous historic document concludes, *Data per manum nostram in prato quod vocatur Runimed inter Windleshore et Stanes*, do not imply that the king either wrote or sealed the charter; they are merely used to give to it greater weight and force as a royal Act, and perhaps imply that John did actually deliver it with his own hands to the barons.

Prior to the reign of Edward III—when the Black Prince is believed to have affixed to a document words equivalent to his signature—we have no evidence of any member of the royal family being able to write his or her name. Sovereigns of times previous to that of Richard I occasionally made their 'marks' on charters granted by them. The mark—usually cruciform—was placed either before or in the middle of the grantor's name, that name having been already written in by the scribe who penned the charter, and who left space for it. This mark was made probably at the actual time of granting the charter, that is, of giving it—after it had been publicly read aloud—to the grantee. King Cadwalla in one of his charters expressly states his own inability to write his name, in words, which, when translated, read, 'With my own hand, on account of ignorance of letters, I have made and written the sign of the cross.' However, the instances of post-Saxon kings corroborating their charters with the sign of the cross, made either by themselves or by the charter-writer, are very few in number.

The method I intend to adopt in presenting the reader with specimens of the handwriting of successive English sovereigns, and in some instances of their children, from the time of Edward III to the present day, is to preface each example of writing with a few words, giving, if undated, its approximate date, explaining the circumstances under which it was written, and pointing out any special feature of interest it may contain.

In order to make this volume 'useful' as well as 'curious,' I have given examples of all the forms I have met with of the signatures of English sovereigns. Prior to Henry VIII, the same king often altered considerably the form of his signature; and by giving examples of those various forms I hope the volume may be a guide to those who endeavour either to gauge the authenticity of a document professing to bear a particular royal autograph, or to fix the actual reign to which belongs an instrument that might, from the signature upon it, equally well be of the reigns of Henry IV, Henry V, or Henry VI, or of Edward IV or Edward V.

EDWARD THE 'BLACK PRINCE'

THE only portion of writing extant which is supposed to have been executed by the Black Prince is the curious signature appended to a writ dated at Angoulême in 1370, addressed by him, as Earl of Chester, to the custodians of his seal, directing them to prepare his letters patent for settling a pension upon a certain John de Esquet as a reward for faithful service. About the document itself there is no feature of especial importance. I do not, therefore, propose to give a facsimile of more than the concluding words of it: *Homout. Ich Dene.* To these words attaches the highest

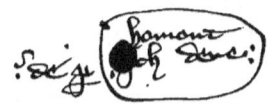

interest, since there is little doubt that they were written by the prince himself, and used by him in the place of his signature to the writ. The 'mottoes'—for such they are—appear, it will be remembered, on the prince's tomb at Canterbury, and in the instructions for his funeral he directs that his body shall be borne to the grave preceded by banners bearing these words. The document, of which we give a translation below, is dated six years before his death, when he was in the fortieth year of his age. His health was then already beginning to fail, and his former magnanimous disposition so far altering as to allow him to consent to the massacre of the vanquished inhabitants of Limoges.

'Edward, eldest son of the King of France and England, Prince of Aquitaine and Wales, Duke of Cornwall, Earl of Chester, Seigneur of Biscay, and

Castre d'Ordiales, to our dear and well-beloved Sir Richard de Stafford, Sir Piers de . . . . . , and John de Heurteworth, greeting. Whereas, in consideration of the good service which our beloved and faithful John de Esquet has done, and will for the future do, for us, we have given and granted him 50 marks sterling by the year during his life, to take at our Exchequer of Chester by the hands of our Chamberlain there for the time being, he doing such loyal homage to us as we have received from him on this side of the sea. We will that upon this our gift and grant aforesaid, you, John de Heurteworth, do issue unto him our letters patent under our seal in your custody, with such others as appertain and are sufficient for him. And these letters shall be your warrant for the same. Given under our privy seal in our city of Angoulême the 25th day of April, 1370[1].'

With regard to the interpretation of the mottoes, *Homout* [Hochmuth] is generally taken to be 'high courage.' The story of the prince adopting as his motto the words *Ich Dene* (I serve)—the words found beneath the plume of ostrich feathers on the helmet of the King of Bavaria as he lay slain on the field of Cressy—is too well known to need more than passing mention.

[1] Original in Latin. Public Record Office.

III

RICHARD II

OF Richard II's signature we have undoubted examples, though they are excessively rare. Internal evidence—the mention of Michael de la Pole as Earl of Suffolk—in the first of the three documents bearing his signature, of which facsimiles are given here, fixes it as belonging to the year 1386, twelve months before the king completed his majority. It is a grant by Richard to the Prioress of Saint Magdalen, at Bristol, of a tun of Gascony wine, to be handed over to her every Christmas at the port of that town. The king here signs his name in English.

Translation of the document referred to above. Original in French. Signature only in the King's handwriting. Public Record Office. See facsimile on following page.

'By the King.

'Well-beloved and faithful. Whereas we of our special grace have given and granted to our well-beloved in God, Elizabeth, Prioress of Saint Magdalen, near our town of Bristol, a tun of red wine of Gascony, to have and take yearly during the term of her life at the Feast of Christmas, in our said town of Bristol, by the hand of our Chief Butler for the time being. We command you that you issue to the said Elizabeth our letters patent for the same, under our great seal in due form. Given under our signet at our Castle of Bristol, the 26th day of July.

'RICHARD.'

Addressed—

'To our well-beloved and faithful Michael de la Pole, Earl of Suffolk, our Chancellor.'

Somewhat more than a mere signature occurs upon a letter written by Richard, in 1389[1], ordering William of Wykeham, the famous Bishop of Winchester, who was his Chancellor, to deliver the great seal to one or other of four persons named, in order that it might be affixed to certain documents concerning a process between the Earl of Salisbury and John Montague, his brother: This done, to take it back and keep it. The letter bears date at Havering, in Essex, on November 15, 1389, and is signed 'Le Roy R.S. sau[n]z dep[ar]tyr'—the King, Richard the Second [wills it to be done] without fail. A facsimile of this signature is given on the plate which stands as frontispiece to this volume.

Another example of this form of Richard's signature, 'le Roy R. S.,' occurs on a document belonging to the year 1397[2]. French is the language of the document to which this signature is appended. There is nothing especially interesting in the document itself, which is written by a professional scribe in the ordinary hand of the period, so that it will be sufficient to give a facsimile of the king's signature alone. The instrument sets

---

[1] Original at the Public Record Office amongst the Collection of Royal Autographs.
[2] British Museum. Cotton MSS., Vespasian F. lii. folio 3.

out the particulars of agreement for the restoration of the Castle of Brest to the Duke of Brittany, an incident in the twenty-five years' truce agreed upon between England and France towards the close of Richard's reign, after Charles VI had consented that his daughter Isabella, at that time only eight years of age, should, on completing her twelfth year, become the wife of the English king, if she wished to do so. The signature reads thus:—

IV

HENRY IV

THE specimens of Henry IV's handwriting are more numerous and interesting, since, in one instance, we have a holograph letter of that sovereign. The date of this document must be placed somewhere between the years 1380—when he was first styled Earl of Derby—and 1399, the date of his accession to the Crown. The letter, which also bears Henry's signet seal, is dated at Hertford on August 13. In it the writer directs William Loveney, Clerk of his Wardrobe, to supply 'Jak Davy' with cloth for a gown for his (Davy's) father, in addition to gowns already allowed for himself, his mother, and his wife.

It is difficult with the process at our disposal to give an adequate representation of the seal, which is of red wax, bears a shield charged with an ostrich feather, and has the name 'Derby' across the field.

Translation of the document above referred to. Holograph. Original in French. British Museum, Stow MSS. Facsimile opposite.

'Dear and good friend.—Whereas we have before spoken to you concerning gowns for Jak Davy, his mother, and his wife, I command you also that you deliver to the said Jack sufficient cloth for a gown for his father. And this our letter shall be your warrant. Written at Hertford, the 13th day of August, with our own hand, as will be to you apparent. We command William Loveney, Clerk of our Wardrobe, to do this under our Seal.'

Now comes an example[1] of Henry of Lancaster's writing after his accession

---

[1] Original at the Public Record Office: Collection of Royal Autographs.

IV. Henry the Fourth

to the throne as Henry IV, and of more interest, not only on that account, but as furnishing a really valuable example of what we may literally term *the King's English* at the very beginning of the fifteenth century—a date at which examples of English, penned by any one, are exceedingly interesting. It occurs upon a formal command to the Archbishop of Canterbury concerning the Queen's dower, at the end of which Henry has written:—

'W[i]t[h]al min trew hert, worchipfull and well beloved cosin, I grete yow ofte well and you, next God, I thonke of that good hele that I am inne, for so I may well, w[i]t[h]out saying so. Reverent and well beloved cosin, I send yow a bille for that Quene, towchyng her dower, wych I pray yow micht be sped, and ye scholl do us bothe gret ese ther inne. Wherefor we woll thonk yow w[i]t[h]al oure hert.

'Your trewe

'son HENRYE.'

This most interesting example of royal penmanship is reproduced in exact facsimile upon the frontispiece plate.

We have other specimens of Henry's handwriting after his accession to the throne, though none so long or so curious as those noted. One is upon a petition addressed to him by a Canon of Windsor on the subject of an obstructed right-of-way. The document is interesting in itself from the glimpse it gives us at a part of the royal borough at the commencement of the fifteenth century, and shows the usual form of the king's signature.

'H. R. We have granted it for him.'

Translation of the document above referred to. Original in French. Public Record Office.

'To our most dread and sovereign Lord, our Lord the King. Most humbly prays your poor Chaplain and continual Orator, Simon Marcheford, Canon of your most honourable College of Windsor, that whereas he and his predecessors have before this time had a garden extending from their house along the side of your ancient hall in your Castle of Windsor so far as the old great chamber, together with a little gate and the key [*le clos*] belonging to it, near the "pulletrie" there, to enable them to come and go freely at all times. This gate is now barred and closed by your officers of the said "pulletrie," to the great discomfort of your said Chaplain, who can no longer bring in his victuals that way for the reason aforesaid. May it please your grace to grant to the said petitioner and his successors the key [*les clos*] and gates aforesaid, so that he may have free ingress and egress through the same in form aforesaid. For God and in the way of charity.'

V

HENRY V

THERE is a good deal of Henry V's writing extant at the present day. Amongst the examples are some tolerably long letters, which show a very skilful power of expression. These are particularly interesting; since—with the exception of the documents before noticed, penned by Henry IV as Earl of Derby and king—they are the earliest examples of royal holograph letter-writing we have. Two of these are written whilst he was Prince of Wales, and are addressed to his father, Henry IV. The first congratulates him on the 'blissid sacrament of mariage,' which he (Henry IV) has concluded with Joan of Navarre, so that the letter belongs to the year 1402, when the writer was but fourteen years of age. He regrets that he was not present at the ceremony; his absence was evidently caused by the existence of the jealousy and suspicion with which Henry IV constantly regarded his youthful heir. The frank and open-hearted strain of the letter leaves us in no doubt about the genuineness of the grief which the boy says he feels at exclusion from his father's presence.

Transcript of the document above referred to. Holograph. Original in English, Public Record Office. See facsimile (1) *on page* 21, *which shows the concluding portion of the letter, commencing at* '*therefore my sovereyne lorde*,' *&c.*[1]

'In all wyse my sovereyne lorde I recoma*n*dde me to you*re* moste noble grace wyghte alle the lowlinesse that any s*u*bgit kan thenkke or devise.

---

[1] The words are written by the prince with numerous abbreviations; the letters supplied to make the words intelligible to ordinary readers are printed in italics.

Ande as you lieste my sov*er*eyne lorde to lete me youre most hu*m*ble liege ma*n* to have knowleche be yowr gracious lettris of the pees and mariage co*n*cludid, the whyche Godde knowyht I have desirid as herttyly as ever dide any poore creature, and that for Goddis worshipp and your moste noble herttis ese. And also for the sov*er*eyne gladnesse and co*m*forte that we yowre trwe pepil have and wyht*e* Goddis mercy shalle have in the lyklynesse of successione of your bodily heyrys y^t lorde thankke yow y^t is verray pees, ande wyhte all the hu*m*blesse that any s*u*bgit kan thankke hys sovereyne lorde, I thankke you my moste gracious sov*er*eyne lorde. Ande there as hyt lykyd yowre hynesse to wryte in zowr*e* forseid gracious lettris y^t ye p*ur*pose the time of youre mariage as sone aftir the feste of the trinite as convenable time comyhte, in the beste tyme of the yer I beseche Godde. And trwly my sov*er*eyne lorde, but if youre hyncsse hadde commanddid me the quarie if I myht have be [been] to Goddis worship, and yourys at that blessid gladde mariage I wolde, for no thyng be thennys but Godde, blissid mote he be, wille not that I have in thys worde [world] y^t y^t I most desired of, the whyche to see that joyfulle day of your mariage haht ben on. Besechyng you my sov*er*eyne lorde to have in yowre noble remembraunce wyhte what conclusion of reste I dep*ar*tid last owte of yowre graciouse presence ande after that I have demended me syhte I kam in to thys youre reaume ande wyhte Goddis grace shalle to my lyvys ende lyk as I truste to Godde youre hu*m*ble lyge man, <u>cousin Chaucer</u>, hahte pleinly enformed youre hynesse or this time. Also my sov*er*eyne lorde whanne I was on the grette see I made awowe after time I were onys in youre reaume of Engelande I sholde no see [sea] passe, —save on pilgrimage, unto [until] I hadde be [been] at Seint Jamys, ande for that cause whanne I was at youre toun of Calays for the grete desir I hadde to see the prosperite of your most dredde ande noble p*er*sone I wentte strehte fro thennys to your most gracious pr*e*sence for if I hadde goone in to your reaume of Engelande I myhte not have come in to Normandie to [till] my pilgrimage hadde be doo [done]. Ande therefore my sovereyne lorde wyht all the humblesse that any subgit kan thenkke or devise I beseche your hynesse to take not to displesaunsse my nowhte comyng, for Godde knowhte I ne feyne noone no colour seke. Besechyng Godde in all wyse my sovereyne lorde to save ande kepe you body and sowle ande sendde you in thys blissid sacrament of mariage, joye, p*r*osperite

(1) Specimen of Henry V's Handwriting when 14 years of age.

(2) Letters of Henry V written in 1411.

V. Henry the Fifth

longe to endure wyhte heyrys of your body to hys blissid worshyp ande yourys in singuler comforte off all youre trewe pepyll of the whyche I am on [one] ande ever shall be. Wryten att Waltham the vj day of Juin.

'Youre humble subgit and trwe ligeman,

'H. W.'¹

Addressed—

'To the Kyng my Sovereyne Lorde.'

The second letter from Prince Henry to his father is written when the former jealousies had, at least to great extent, subsided, and when the prince was in the enjoyment of his father's trust and friendship. The letter is written from Southampton, and with it is sent a muster-roll of the soldiers of the companies under the command of his 'brother of Bedford²,' and other captains. The companies here referred to were probably being dispatched to France, and the date of the letter may be safely fixed as 1411. At this time Henry IV was permitted by the more settled state of affairs at home to revive the old hostile feeling between France and England, so that he was able to send military aid to help the Duke of Burgundy's party in its struggle for power against the party of the Duke of Orleans. The following year, however, he listened to the more advantageous proposal of the Orleanists, and—withdrawing his friendship from the Burgundians—sent over fresh men and supplies to help their cause. The domestic allusions in the letter are exceedingly curious. The lady to whom he refers as his 'cousin of York' is obviously Joan de Holland, widow of Edmund of Langley, fifth son of Edward III, who died in 1402.

Transcript of the document above referred to. Holograph. Original in English, Public Record Office. See facsimile (2) on page 21, which shows the passages relating to 'my cosne of York' and 'Tiptot', and also the signature.

'My soverain lord and fader, I recomande me to yowr good and gracieux lordship as humbly as I can, desiring to heere as good tydynggess of you and of your hye estat as ever did leige man of his soverain lord. And,

---

[1] Probably for 'Henricus Walliae,' or 'Henry Prince of Wales.'
[2] John, Duke of Bedford, second son of Henry IV.

sir, I trust to God that ye shal have now a companie comyng wit*h* my brother of Bedford that ye shal like wel in good feith as hit is do me wite, neve*r*thelatter, my brother's mainy [retinue] have I seyn, which is right a tal meyny [retinue]. And so schal ye se of thaym that be of your other captaines leding, of which I sende you al the names in a rolle be the berer-of this. Also so, sir, blessid be God, of the good and gracieux tydingg*es* that ye have liked to send me word of be Herford your messager which were the gladdist that eve*r* I mygt heve next your welfare, be my trouth, and, sir, with Godde's grace I shal sende all thise ladies as ye have commandid me, in al hast, beseching you of your lordship that I mygt wite how that ye wolde that my cosine of York shuld reule her, whether she shuld be barbid[1] or not as I have wreten to you, my soverain lord afore this time. And, sir, as touching Tiptot he shal be delive*r*ed in al hast, for ther lakkith no thing but shipping, which, with Goddes grace, shall be so ordeined for that he shal not tary. Also, sir, blessid be God, your gret ship the Grace Dieu is even as redy and is the fairest that eve*r* man saugh, I trowe in good feith. And this same day therle of Devonshir my cosin maad his moustre [muster] in her and al other have her [there] moustre [mustered (?)] the same tyme that shall go to ye see [sea]. And, sir, I trowe ye have on [one] comyng toward you as glad as any man can be as fer as he shewith, that is the King of Scotts, for he thanketh God that he shal mow shewe be expe*r*ience thentente of his good will be the suffrance of your good lordship. My soverain lord, more can I not write to your hynesse at this tyme, but yt eve*r* I beseche you of your good and gracieux lordship as be my trouth my witting [knowingly] willingly I shal neve*r* deserve the contrary, that woot God, to whom I pray, to send yow al yt yowr hert desireth to his plaisance. Writen in your town of Hampton the xiiij day of May.

'Your trewe and humble liege man and sone

'H. G.[2]'

After Prince Henry's accession to the throne, we have a portion of a letter written by him whilst in France, probably in the year 1419, apparently to the person left in charge of home affairs whilst the king prosecuted his wars

---
[1] *i.e.* dressed as a widow.
[2] Probably ' Henricus Gwalliae,' or for ' Henry Prince de Galle.'

Letter of Henry V, written in 1419.

Furthermore I woll that ye wuche Saueth, in Especial wyth the Chauncelleir touchyng my coyn of my Finchyngland and my coin of Ireland and that ye se it at goode ordinance for my wourchipper and frendys, for the Duc of Irland and for alle the remanent of my prisoners of France and also for the Erle of Scotland. For as I am fully enformed by a man of tryst that met with the kyng that they Schold bee a man of the Suar of France before & man of tryst therefore there Send Acoord betwyx the Duc of Albany, that the next somer before of France in Scotland Acord betwyx the Duc of Albany, and also that they Schold bryng in the manner of Scotland As fungrez hit be may, and also that they Schold founden Essex to the Eastryng Bay presely of the Duc of Orliance. And therfore be ye ware as welle of the remanent of my forsen prisoners that ben in the castell of Fortryngay be welle suer kept Soyng to robyn & Iare or to any other ordynaunce for it in Eythe be lesse suertee than in thecastell.

I woll that the Duc of Orliance be kept stille within the castell of Fortryngay & that in no wyse he come from that .... of alle the remanent suche as ye thynkyth abroad. The French prisoners he refers to were, no doubt, those taken four years before at the battle of Agincourt. His suspicions are, we see, aroused that the Duke of Orleans is endeavouring to carry on an intrigue with Scotland, so he directs the continuance of his close confinement at Pontefract, whither he had been removed from Windsor; he did not regain his liberty till 1440. The last ten years of his confinement were passed in the Tower of London, where he employed much of his time in sonnet-writing. Amongst his compositions are three written in English, and expressed in a way which shows that during his captivity he had acquired a very perfect knowledge of the language. James I—the King of Scotland here spoken of by King Henry, and alluded to by him in the letter to Henry IV last quoted—had been a prisoner in England since 1405, and was liberated in 1424; he, too, has left us specimens of poetic composition written whilst in prison.

Transcript of the document referred to above. Holograph original in English. British Museum, Cotton MSS. Vespasian F. iii. folio 5. Facsimile opposite.

'Furthremore I wold that ye comend with my brothre, with the chanceller, with my cosin of Northumbrelond and [with] my cosin of Westmeland; and that ye set a gode ordinance for my north marches, and specially for the Duc de Orlians, and for all the remanant of my prisoners of France and also for the k[ing] of Scotelond, for, as I am secrely enfourmed by a man of ryght notable estate in this lond, that there hath ben a man of the Duc of Orliance in Scotland and accorded with the Duc of Albany that this next somer he schal bryng in the maumet [puppet] of Scotlond to sturre what he may, and also that ther schold be founden weys to the havyng awey specialy of the Duc of Orlians and also of the k[ing], as welle as of the remanant of my forsayd prysoners; that God do defende. Wherefore I wolle that the Duc de Orliance be kept stille within the Castil of Pontfret with owte goyng to Robertis place or to any othre disport, for it is bettre he lak his disport then we were disceyved. Of alle the remanant dothe as ye thenketh.'

One more specimen of Henry's handwriting may be given, in the words with which he grants a petition addressed to him by a suitor for the continuance of an annuity granted by his late brother, Thomas Duke of

Handwriting of the Kings and Queens of England

Clarence, who was slain at Baugy in 1421; the document therefore shows us the king's handwriting but a short time before his death. The allusions to the 'Castle of Hawardyn' give the document a present-day interest.

Translation of the document above referred to. Original in French. Public Record Office. The words 'R. H. In the fo[r]me and man[er]e that our brother's l[ett]res p[ur]poten whil us lust,' *only in the King's handwriting.*

'To our Lord the King.

'Humbly prays your suitor John Kyngesley Esquire, That whereas his most dread Lord, Thomas Duke of Clarence, your brother, whom God assoil, by his letters patent granted to your said suppliant an annual rent [of ten pounds during] the life of your said suppliant from the rents issues profits and revenues of his Castle and Lordship of Hawardyn within the county of Chester[1] by the hands of his receiver there for the time being at the feast of Saint Mi .... as in the same letters patent more fully is contained. The which Castle and Lordship aforesaid, after the death of the aforesaid Duke, have come into your hands by reason that the said Duke died without heir of his body .... to give and grant to your said suppliant the said ten pounds to be taken annually for the term of his life at the feasts abovesaid of the said issues rents profits and revenues of the Castle and Lordship abovesaid by the hands of ...... according to the form of the letters patent aforesaid. Any gift or grant by you to your said suppliant before this time made notwithstanding. For God and as a work [of Charity].'

Signatures are given on the next page (in two forms) of the king's brother, Humphry Duke of Gloucester, Regent and Chamberlain of England during

---

[1] For certain legal purposes the county of Flint was annexed to the county of Chester.

V. Henry the Fifth

part of the minority of Henry VI; of Cardinal Beaufort; and of Jacquetta of Luxemburg, wife of the Regent Bedford. These are taken from documents in the Collection of Royal Autographs at the Public Record Office.

H. Chambellan of England.

Homfrey.

Cardinal Henry Beaufort, Bishop of Winchester, half-brother of Henry IV.

Jaquetta.

VI

HENRY VI

THOUGH Henry VI's signature—in its short form 'R. H.'—appears on a large number of signed bills and other documents of a like nature, as well as on petitions which he grants, yet no letter of any length certainly in his handwriting is known to exist. Mr. Maxwell Lyte has, however, kindly called my attention to the following words—'R. H. nous avou[n]s grau[n]te C. marc[ks]'—written by this king on a document of the year 1437, and to an interesting example of his writing, which shows that at the age of sixteen he made use of a wood-block stamp of his name. Facsimiles of these are given on the frontispiece plate. All the circumstances connected with the use of the wood-block are of great interest. In the first place, it is an early instance of the use of such stamps, which were then but slightly known. A few instances of their use are recorded; but only on the Continent, and by Notaries-public, or other officials who had occasion to make very frequent use of their names. Secondly, it is singular to find a boy of sixteen thus saving his labour in writing, especially when the words immediately preceding and following it are *penned* by him. I am inclined to accept Mr. Lyte's suggestion that the use of the *stamp* was really nothing more than a boyish freak: the wood-block simply a toy!

Two of these granted petitions—each having some internal interest—are given in this volume. They are both written in English, and are fair samples of the spelling and composition of the period—A.D. 1446-7. The first is addressed by the Colleges of Eton and Cambridge to the king, praying him to appoint a commission for purchasing books, vestments,

VI. Henry the Sixth.

&c. This commission, they beg, may consist of one of the king's chaplains, the king's stationer, 'and othere suche as ben connynge and have undirstondynge in suche matiers.'

Original in English. Public Record Office. 'R. H.' only in the King's handwriting. See facsimile at the side, which shows the King's signature and part of the first line of the document.

'R. H.

'Unto the Kinge oure Soverauyn Lorde.

'Besechethe mekely youre humble and trewe Orators the Provostes and Felowes of youre two Colages Roialle of Eton and Cambrigge, that forasmoche as thei bene of your Royall Funducione nowe late foundede and newe growynge and as yitte not so sufficianntely storede in suche thinges as in verre trouthe of necessete and honeste moste nedes be hadde, as bokes for divine service and for theire lybraryes and theire studyes, vestymentes and othere onourementes, whiche thinges may not be hadde withe owte grete and diligente laboure be longe processe and right besy Inquisione.

'Please it to your most noble grace to yeve in specialle commaundement and charge to Maister Richarde Chestre oon of youre Chapellaynes that he take to hyme suche mene as shalle be seene to hym expedient and profitable and in especialle John Pye your Stacionere of London and other suche as bene connynge and have undirstondynge in suche matiers, chargynge hem and eueriche of hem to be assistant and helping hym with alle here diligence atte alle suche tymes as thei shalle be requirede be the seide Maistere Richarde for to laboure effectually, inquere and diligently inserche, in alle places that bene undir youre obeysaunse to gete knowleche where suche bokes onourmentes and othere necessaries for youre seide

Colages maybe foundene to selle. Grauntinge unto the forsaide Maistere Richarde youre fulle noble lettres patentz to be made in due fowrme undir youre grete sealle for to make suche bokes and ornementes where evere thei be foundene to selle and make theyme to be lawfully and reasonably be praysede be mene of gode conscience; and that doone, it be lefulle to hym to bye take and receive all suche goodes afore eny othere manne for the expedicione and profite of youre seide Colages, satisfying to the owners of suche godes suche pris as thei may resonably accorde and agree soo that he may have the ferste choise of alle suche goodes afore eny othere manne, and in especialle of all manner bokes ornementes and other necessaries as nowe late were perteyninge to the Duke of Gloucestre. And of youre habundaunt grace like it youe to charge streitely the seide Maistere Richarde that he doo all his diligence, cesse not but alwey contynewe his laboure unto suche tyme that youre seide Colages be sufficiently stuffide of suche bokes and necessaries as is afore reherside takinge the forseide Maistere Richarde his servantes and theyme that bene assistaunt and helpars to hym in this occupacione unto youre graciouse protectione duringe the tyme of his laboure for youre seide Colages. And we shalle ever pray God for youe.'

The second example of Henry VI's signature is on a petition addressed to him by Robert Coksale, a vestment maker of London, which evidently relates to the subject of the last-quoted document, since, here, the petitioner complains of his inability to obtain payment for 'certayn vestmentes of white damask of div[er]ses sortes rychely embrowedered,' supplied for Eton College and for the King's 'Colage Roiale of Our Lady and Saint Nicolas of Cambrygge.' These he had supplied to one John Langton, Chancellor of Cambridge, and subsequently Bishop of St. Davids. Langton, however, died within fifteen days of the appointment to St. Davids, hence Coksale's difficulty in obtaining payment for his goods supplied.

Original in English. Public Record Office. '*R. H.*' *only in the King's handwriting. Facsimile opposite, which shows the King's signature and part of the first line of the document.*

  'R. H.

    'To the Kyng our Sov[er]ayn lord.

 'Besecheth mekely your humble Oratour Robert Coksale, Vestment maker of your Cite of London, That whereas Maister John Langton, late Bisshop

VI. Henry the Sixth

of Saint Davids did get your seid oratour to make certayn Vestmentes of white damask of div[er]ses sortes rychely embrowedered, aswell for your colage Roiale of our lady of Eton as for your Colage Royall of our lady and Saint Nicolas of Cambrygge, for the which Vestments there is due unto your said Oratour ccxli^{li} xix^s iij^d, as it appereth more clerly by a scedule of parcelles to this bill annexed, of the which scedule the seid Bysshop hadde the doub... to have shewed it unto yor highnesse for the payment of the seid some, whereof as yit he in no wise may have no payment. And in case the seid Vestmentes should been delivered fro your seid Oratour which as yit been in his kepyng without payment for the same it shuld be to his utter destruction and undoyng That it myght please you therefer of your most speciall Grace to considre these premisses and also how that your seid Oratour is gretely endetted to diuerses persones for the grete part of the stuf for the seid Vestmentes and to graunt unto your seed Oratour for his more suerte by your l[ett]res patentes that he his heirs executers or assignes may have and kepe the seid Vestmentes unto the tyme that your seid Oratour his heirs executours or assignes have been fully payed content or agreed for the seid Vestmentes of the seid some of ccxli^{li} xix^s iij^d without any interrupcion lette or disturbaunce of you or of any of yo[u]r officers or Ministres or elles of any other persone whatsomever. And he shall pray God for you.'

> 'The King g[r]aunted this bille at Newbury the xxx day of Aoust the yer of his Regne xxv. Present, my lord Bisshop of Sarum and my lord Say.'

Yet another form of Henry VI's signature occurs upon a curious document preserved amongst the muniments of Eton College. It is appended to certain alterations in what is generally known as the king's 'will': the alterations relate to the building of the College Chapel, and very full extracts from them are given by Mr. Maxwell Lyte, in his *History of Eton College*. By the kindness of the publishers, Messrs. Macmillan & Co., we are enabled to give below a representation of the signature from the wood-block used in Mr. Lyte's book.

VII

EDWARD IV AND HIS QUEEN, ELIZABETH WYDEVILE

FEW individuals, or bodies corporate, had greater reason to view with apprehension the overthrow of the House of Lancaster, and the victory of Edward Duke of York at Mortimer's Cross, than had the College of Eton—the foundation, and especially favoured foundation, of Henry VI. Mr. Maxwell Lyte, in his history of the College before mentioned, states that the Provost and Canons acted with more wisdom than courage, in at once submitting themselves to the victorious party. They went forward, without delay, to meet Edward on his march eastwards, towards London, and it would seem, by so doing obtained from him a promise of protection, which probably allayed their uneasiness.

This interesting document may still be seen in the College Library, and furnishes a unique example of the future king's signature just prior to his accession. The wording is so interesting—the phrase by which Edward describes himself—that we make no excuse for here quoting its commencement.

'Be it knowen that We, Edward, by the grace of God, of Englande Fraunce and Irland, vray and just heire, Duc of York, Erl of the March and Ulvestre, have by thees our lettres taken and receyved the Provoste and felaship of the Collage of Eyton into our defense and saveguard.'

The document concludes by warning all persons to in no wise vex or spoil those whom the duke had thus taken under his protection, and is signed as shown above.

Subsequent history shows us that the Provost and Fellows found that Edward did not keep his word, and they, like other Lancastrians, suffered loss of revenue; but into this we must not enter.

When this series of papers appeared in the pages of the *Leisure Hour* some few years ago, I was compelled to state that no connected sentence written by Edward IV was known to be extant, though, as is the case with respect to Henry VI, numerous specimens of his signature, 'E. R.,' were known to occur on formal documents. I am now, by the kindness of my friend Mr. Maxwell Lyte, the Deputy-Keeper of the Records, enabled to present to the reader both the signature of Edward when Duke of York, already given, and also (on the plate facing this page) a facsimile of a long sentence, composed by the 'Sun of York[1],' and written in his own hand. It occurs on a document lately come to light, which is a writ to the Chancellor ordering a commission to be sent to the Mayor of Bristol, and others, for the trial of those who had committed riot in the west of England. It reads:—' Cosyn yff ye thynke ye schult have a warrant thys, our wryten, shal soffysse on to [until] ye may have on made, in dew forme. We pray you hyt Fayle not to be don.' One of the documents, which bears the usual 'E. R.,' has considerable historic interest, and is therefore worthy of pretty full quotation. It is the minute of the proceedings at a council held in the English camp near Peronne in 1475, at which Edward IV empowered certain persons in his retinue to treat with Louis XI of France for a peace which, it will be remembered, was ultimately agreed upon.

This document—which also bears the signatures of Edward's two brothers, Richard Duke of Gloucester (afterwards Richard III) and George Duke of Clarence, who was attainted and murdered in 1477—recites that the king, attended by a numerous company of nobles, was, on August 25, 1475, 'in his felde beside a village called Seyntre within Vermondose a litelle from Peronne.' Here 'certeyne offres and requestes were made unto his highnes be [by] the Frensshe Kyng for a trewx and abstinence of werre and other intelligences to be had betwixt theme both con[sider]yng the povertie of his armye, the nygh approchyng wynter and smale assistence of his allies;' whereupon Edward 'called thane and there before

---

[1] Original in Public Record Office: Collection of Royal Autographs.

By the King

Right Reverend fadre in god right trusty and entierly beloved Cosyn. We grete you wele And for so muche as we ben
enformed that many undisposed persones have of late secretly by untrue feyned & subtile meanes labored to excite a
[illegible] simple people of oure Towne of [illegible] & [illegible] to [illegible] [illegible] meanes
of [illegible] & [illegible] [illegible] ayenst oure honoure & ayenst the Comune wele of oure lande & oure
[illegible] and peax. We therfore wol and desire you that incontinent after the sight of these ye doo make oure
Commission of Oyer determiner directed to John [illegible] Maire of oure saide Towne of [illegible]
Richard [illegible] oon of oure Justices Thomas [illegible] oure Sergeant at the lawe William [illegible] [illegible]
[illegible] William [illegible] John [illegible] Thomas [illegible] & William [illegible] [illegible] [illegible]
may be proceded to the punicion of the saide [illegible] [illegible] [illegible] [illegible] [illegible] [illegible]
[illegible] [illegible] Warrant [illegible] [illegible] under oure Signet at oure Castell of [illegible] the
seconde day of Decembre

Cosyn yt ye ~~[illegible]~~ thynke ye schall have
a Warrant [illegible] and [illegible]
ye may have hit made in dew forme the
pray you that thys not fayle [illegible]

VII. Edward the Fourth and his Queen, Elizabeth Wydevile

his highnes, the lord Howard Maister of the Rolles Deane of his Chapelle, and Thomas Selynger,' whom he charged to 'goo unto the said Frensshe Kyng, or suche as he shuld depute for his partie, geving theme power and auctorite,' and also charged Lord Howard and Thomas Selynger to agree with him or them 'under fourme folowing,' that is to say: 'if the Frensshe Kyng wolle bynde him, his cuntries and subgets, to paie within 15 daies unto oure soveraigne lord lxxv m^l scutes and at Ester then next folowing xxv m^l scutes and at Michelmas thane next folowing other xxv m^l scutes and soo continuelly forthe yereley l m^l scutes during their bothe lyves. And also if the said Frensshe Kyng wolle doo marie his sone, called the Delphyne, at his charge and cost to his furst or the second of oure said soveraigne lorde's doughters indowing her with lx m^l pounds of rent yerely, after the estimacione of Fraunce; that thane thei shuld bynd oure said soveraigne lord to withdrawe his armie, incontinent upone the receipt of the said lxxv m^l scutes into Englond, and to bynde hyme to lay plegges soo to doo.'

Besides this, it was further agreed that the two kings 'shuld make a private amyte betwixt them bothe byndyng theme to a mutuelle assistence in case any oftheme bothe were be [by] their subgetts wronged or disobeied. And also to make betwixt theme both a treux and abstinence of werre with intercourse of merchaundises for their cuntres and subgetts to endure for vij yere next folowing.' The king's signature, thus:
appears at the head of the document; those of Gloucester and Clarence as given below.

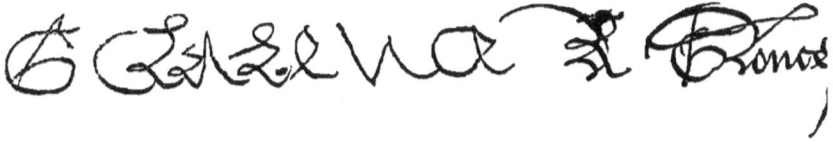

Elizabeth Wydevile, the wife of Edward IV, is the first English queen of whose handwriting any specimen is known to exist. She was the daughter of Sir Richard Wydevile (by Jacqueline, or Jaquetta, widow of the Regent Bedford), and married Edward IV on May 1, 1464.

The example of her signature which we give here is appended to a document of some importance, since it goes a good way towards refuting the statement frequently dwelt upon in history, that Henry VII—who, perhaps rightly, possesses a character for carefulness, carried to the degree of meanness—seized his mother-in-law's possessions, and left her without any adequate means of support. In the following, we see a receipt given by Elizabeth, the Queen Dowager, for the arrears of a pension of £400 a year allowed her by her son-in-law.

Original in English. Public Record Office. Signature only in Queen's handwriting.

'Be hyt remembyrd that I Quene Elyzabethe late wyffee to the exelent prynce, Kyng Edward the iiijth, have reseyvede the xxi day of May the vjth yere of King Herry the viith of John Lord Denham tresorer of Ynglond be the handdes of Thomas Stolys, on [one] of the reseyte, xxx^{li} in party of payment of CC^{li} due to me at ester last past as hyt aperyth be my annuete grauntyd be the Kyng. In wytnes wher of I have endosyd thys byll wythe my hand the day and yere above said.

'ELYSABETH.'

SPECIMEN OF THE HANDWRITING OF ELIZABETH WYDEVILL, WIFE OF EDWARD IV.

VIII

EDWARD V

ELIZABETH'S unfortunate son—though his reign lasted little more than a couple of months—has left us several varieties of his signature—all, however, attached to purely formal documents.

In May, 1483, he signs (and the Duke of Gloucester countersigns) a proclamation to the Sheriff of Middlesex, commanding those in his county who were in the enjoyment of lands of a certain value, to appear before him and receive the honour of knighthood—which, it must be remembered, at that period, and, indeed, for some time after, was regarded rather as a burthen than an honour, entailing, as it did, the performance of a variety of costly and troublesome services. The document has no internal interest, and so the representation of the king's signature is all that need be given here. Edward was only thirteen years of age when he wrote the letters shown in the margin.

We also find, at the British Museum, a strip of parchment, apparently cut from a document, on which the king's signature occurs in full and is written in Latin [1].

[R. EDWARDUS QUINTUS.]

[1] British Museum, Cotton MSS., Vesp. F. xiii, Folio 53.

Another parchment, the date of which may be fixed as early in June, 1483, deserves more attention for its own sake, and is therefore printed below in full: it shows us a completely different form of the king's signature. The document is a warrant to the Lord Chancellor to issue writs for a Parliament to meet at Westminster on the 25th of June 'next comyng,' which introduces us to a noteworthy historic fact, namely, that it was the intention of Edward—or, rather, we should say, of those who ruled him—to summon a Parliament; there is no evidence, however, that the writs for this Parliament were ever issued in accordance with the royal warrant.

Original in English. Public Record Office. See facsimile at the side, which shows the King's signature and part of the first line of the document.

'R. E.

'Edward by the g[r]ace of God Kyng of England and of Fraunce and lord of Irlond. To the rev[er]ent fader in God John Bisshop of Lincoln our chaunceller gretyng. Forasmoche as We for c[er]tain causes and considera-[ci]ons suche as sp[eci]ally move us and conc[er]ne the wele of us and of all this our Realme and subiectis of the same have by thadwys [the advice] of our counseill ordeyned and appoynted a parlement to be holden at Westmynster and to begynne there the xxv day of Juyn next comyng. We wull and charge you that under our great seall ye do make our writtes for the callyng and somons of our said Parlement to the said day and place in due fourme and in suche case accustumed. And this our writyng shalbe unto you sufficient Warant and discharge in this behalf.'

The murder of the king and his brother happened three days before the date here fixed for the assembly of this Parliament.

SPECIMEN OF THE HANDWRITING OF RICHARD III, WRITTEN IN 1483.

IX

RICHARD III

THERE is a good deal of the handwriting of Richard III preserved to the present day. Two letters of his are of particular interest, since the wording of each is expressive of the impetuous character of the writer. In the earlier of the two—dated at Lincoln on October 12, 1483, three months after his coronation—he commands the Lord Chancellor to send him, with all haste, his great seal, the possession of which is rendered necessary for carrying out his schemes against the Duke of Buckingham. But the formal language of the letter, written by some careful official, in nowise expressed the feelings of the infuriated king, and taking his own pen he has added to it as follows [1]:—

'We wolde most gladly ye camme yourselffe yf that ye may; and yf ye may not We pray you not to fayle but to accomplyshe in all dyllygence oure sayde comawndement to sende Oure Seale incontenent apone the syght heroffe as We trust you with suche as ye trust and the offycers pertenyng to attend with hyt praying you to assertayne us of your newes there. Here, loved be God, ys alle welle and trewly determyned and for to resyste the malysse of hyme that hadde best cawse to be trewe, the Duc of Bokyngame, the most untrewe creature lyvyng whome with Godes Grace We shalle not be long tylle that we wylle be in that partyes and subdewe his malys. We assure you there was never falsse traytor better purvayde for as this berrerre Gloucestre shall shewe you.'

[1] See facsimile on opposite page.

Equally expressive of the king's temper is another letter—undated—also addressed to the chancellor, in which he directs him to prepare in hot haste a pardon for a certain priest.

Original in English. Holograph. Public Record Office. For facsimile, see page 48.

'My lord chauncelere We pray you in alle haste to send to Us a pardone undere Oure Gret Seale to Sir Henry Wode, preste, &c. and this shalbe your W[arrant].

'M[aster] Skypton spede this forthwyth.

'RICARDUS REX.'

Specimen of the Handwriting of Richard III.

Specimen of the Handwriting of Henry VII.

X

HENRY VII

HENRY VII has, perhaps rightly, obtained the character of being careful to the degree of meanness. His carefulness is certainly demonstrated by the extreme pains he took with regard to his household accounts. Two volumes of these are still extant, and a facsimile, showing a portion of a page from one, is given on page 48. Every word on the first four pages of this volume is written by the king. The entries in the remainder of the volume, and throughout the other, are made by a clerk; but Henry checked all the 'totals,' and placed his initials both at the foot and at the top of the page. The items which we see in the facsimile are curious, as showing the king's numerous dealings with large sums of money *in specie*— 'oone bagge of krownes of weyght m^l vj^c xliij' [pounds]—and others of a similar kind.

Transcript of the document above referred to.   Public Record Office.
Facsimile opposite.

'Med.' delyvered to Jhean Heron this xij day of Juyll[y] in oone bagge of Krounes of weyghte m^l vj^c xliij. It[em] delyvered the same day in an other bagge in krownes of weyghte ix^c lxix krownes, whereof delyvered to Pierres Danyelle by Mathieu Baker in advanced for plate a m^l krownes. It[em] delyvered the xix day of Juyll[y] to Jhean Heron in ducatz m^{l}m^{l}m^l ccc xxx^{li}; whereof Lewes de la Fava receyved in sterling money vij^{c}l li xiij^s iiij^d which is discharged in the boke of acompts.

'Me[moran]d[um] delyvered by Sir Thomas Lovelle, in dyvers man[er]s, of gold of beyond the see in Flemysche gold broght by hym from Calais the

50   *Handwriting of the Kings and Queens of England*

xxth day of Juinge aº xixº, the some of viijᶜ li flemysche, which Sʳ Sampson Norton and Nicolas Boveton delyvered hym of the revenuz of Marke and Oye in the marches of Calais.'

Besides demonstrating the king's love of money-making, the study of these books of accounts reveals evidence of some very questionable dealings in the employment of spies. The name of Sir Richard Empson—who, in company with Dudley, another of the king's ministers, suffered on Tower Hill soon after the accession of Henry VIII—appears frequently in connexion with these entries. There are, too, in these books, some curious allusions, under the date 1497, to the rebellion made by Perkin Warbeck, or 'Piers Osebeke,' as he is there generally termed.

The signature given above ('Henricus R.') is a particularly bold example of Henry VII's writing. It occurs on a letter written by him from Woodstock in 1502 to the Venetian Ambassador.

X. Henry the Seventh

By way of comparison we add two other forms of this king's signature :—

TWO FORMS OF HENRY VII'S SIGNATURE.

It may not be out of place to give here an example of the handwriting of the woman through whom Henry VII obtained whatever title he might have had to the throne of England—I mean that of his mother, Margaret Beaufort, great-granddaughter of John of Gaunt. It is written as a postscript to a letter to his Chancellor on business matters, and reads :—' My lord, Y pray yow Y may her of your newes of Flaundyrse. M. Rychmond[1].'

[1] Original at Public Record Office: Collection of Royal Autographs. For facsimile see opposite page.

XI

HENRY VIII AND HIS WIVES

IT would be difficult to find a more interesting specimen of Henry VIII's handwriting than that which is furnished in the following letter to his favourite, Thomas Wolsey—' Myne awne good Cardinall,' as he calls him :—

Holograph. Original at British Museum. Additional MSS. 19,398. 644. Facsimile opposite.

'Myne awne good Cardinall. I recommande me unto you, as hartely as hart can thynke. So it is that by cause wryttyng to me is somewhat tedius and paynefull, therfor the most part off this bysynesses I have commytted to our trusty counseler thys berrer to be declaryd to yow by mowthe, to whyche we wollde you shulde gyff credens. Nevertheles to thys that folowith, I thowght nott best to make hym pryve, nor nonother but you and I, whyche is that I wolde you shuld make good watche on the duke off Suffolke, on the duke of Bukyngam, on my lord off Northetomberland, on my lord off Darby, on my lord of Wylshere and on others whyche you thynke suspecte, to see what they do with thes nwes [news]. No more to you at thys tyme, but *sapienti pauca.* Wryttyne under the hand off your lovying master,

'HENRY R.'

The exact date of this letter is uncertain, but it probably belongs to the year 1519. The writer was then less than thirty years of age, so that the acknowledgement he makes of the tediousness and trouble he finds in writing, must be accounted for by a defective education. The whole style of the letter—its spelling and handwriting—bears this out. The news to which Henry refers may allude to the overtures recently made for a closer alliance with France. It is difficult to assign any particular reason for

LETTER OF HENRY VIII TO CARDINAL WOLSEY.

Myne awne good cardinall I recommande me vnto yow as hartely as hart can thynke / prayeng yow that by cause wrytyng to me is sum what tediius and paynefull therfor the most part off thes bysynesses I have commyttyd to our trusty consseler thys berrar to be declaryd to yow by mouthe to whyche we wolde yow shulde geff credens / neverthelles to thys that folowyth I thought nott best to make hym pryve nor non other but yow and I, whych thys is that I wolde yow shulde make good wache on the duke off suffolke on the duke off bukyngam on my lord off northumberla on my lord off darby on my lord off wylsher and other whyche yow thynke suspecte to see what they do wt thys mater no more to yow at thys tyme but sapienti pauca wryttyn wt the hand off your lovyng master — Henry. R.

XI. Henry the Eighth and his Wives

Henry's suspicion of the nobles mentioned, most of whom were, at least outwardly, enjoying his personal friendship. There is, however, a letter dated in the spring of 1518, from the Pope to the Bishop of Worcester, which gives obscure hints as to a disaffection amongst the nobles; and of this disaffection the shrewd writer of the letter before us may have been cognizant, though he was too good a diplomatist to allow his knowledge to show itself openly.

There will, however, be looked for, and naturally looked for, by the readers of this volume, some example of Henry's handwriting in connexion with the great event in English history with which his reign is associated in the minds of most of us : I mean the Reformation.

This is not the place in which to discuss the motives of the king in his actions with regard to religion, or of his personal faith ; but it is not without interest, and it is certainly instructive, to consider for a moment his declaration of belief, at a period when the Reformation had actually commenced, and had, as we know, at the instigation of those opposed to the suppression of the religious houses, caused a violent outbreak in the northern parts of England —the Pilgrimage of Grace, as it was called. After its suppression, the king's supremacy in spiritual as well as temporal matters seemed more than ever firmly established. Yet in matters of *belief* he appeared willing to make concessions to the popular feeling!

The Articles of Religion, put forward under royal authority in 1536, were criticized by many on account of the omissions therefrom of four of the then recognized seven sacraments ; and Henry so far regarded popular prejudices that he, in February, 1537, called upon the bishops to consider the points of doctrine which justified this omission. Before the close of the bishops' deliberations, the Archbishop of York was able to assure a correspondent that the omitted sacraments would be found in a new edition of the Articles of Religion which would—as a result of those deliberations—be put forward. Although in the month of May, Lord Hussey told Lord Lisle that the episcopate was 'at a point,' yet it was not until July that the new articles appeared, under the title of *The Godly and Pious Institution of a Christian Man*—a work which soon came to be familiarly termed 'the Bishops' Book'—which, as we see, was a very suitable title for it. This was signed by the whole body of those who had deliberated on the question.

It contained an exposition of the Apostles' Creed, the Seven Sacraments, the Ten Commandments, the Lord's Prayer, and the Ave Maria, together with two articles on Justification and Purgatory, which were, with slight verbal differences, reproduced from the articles of the previous year. As we know, this work was printed, issued, and ordered to be read in the churches; but it is also the fact that Henry steered clear of giving a direct approval of all it contained, saying—when asked to do so—that he had not had time to examine it thoroughly. This brings us to the point which our facsimile illustrates. Undoubtedly some part of the outcome of the episcopal deliberations had been submitted to the king *in manuscript*. Here we see the first page of 'Tharticle concernynge the soulles of them whiche be departed from this lyfe,' which is of the highest interest, from the fact that the alterations in the text are in Henry's own handwriting. There can, therefore, be no doubt that, as altered, we have in this article the views which, in 1537, Henry VIII believed, or, at least, thought it prudent to express. A transcript of the whole article—as altered by the king—follows, and with the aid of this no difficulty will be experienced in deciphering the facsimile:—

Original at the Public Record Office. State Papers, Henry VIII. Vol. XII, part 2, No. 401 (3).

'Tharticle concernynge the soulles of them whiche be departed from this lyfe.

'As towchinge the soulles of them whiche be departed, forasmuche as we have no ∧ certaine knolledge of their state, but only as farfourthe as tholye Scripture speaketh of them : therfor we thinke it conveniente that all bishoppes and preachors [*shall*][1] instructe and teache the people commytted unto there spirituall charge, after this manner folowinge. Firste, that the dethe of them, whiche here in this worlde lyved wyckedly, and so departed oute of this lyfe withoute repentaunce, is (as the Scripture saithe) [*very evill, for it is the gate and entree unto everlastinge deathe and dampnation*]. The soulles of them, as it apperithe by thexample of the richeman, of whom S. Luke speaketh in his gospell, [*be in the tormente of hell fyre. They*] be continually in thindignation and wrathe of God, everlastinge deathe gnawith upon them, and hell [*is there*] dwelling place. Their parte is in the lake, that burnethe withe fyre and brymston, which is the seconde deathe. They be allways in an horrible feare of the day of iudgement,

---

[1] By comparison with the facsimile on page 57 it will be seen that the words in italics were all struck out by the king.

PORTION OF A DOCUMENT — 'THE BISHOP'S BOOK' — OF THE PERIOD OF THE REFORMATION
CONTAINING ALTERATIONS IN THE HANDWRITING OF HENRY VIII.

XI. Henry the Eighth and his Wives

when it shalbe saide unto them, Goe ye cursedd into everlastinge fyre, whiche is prepared for the devle and his angelles. And contrarywyse the deathe of the rightuous men is precyous in the sight of our Lorde. And blissed be they that dye in him, for their deathe is the veray gate and entree unto everlastinge lyfe and salvation. Iff they be prevented with deathe yet shall they be in perpetuall reste. The soulles of them be in comforthe and solace, and shall never come to condempnation. Their soulles be in the handes of God, the payne of deathe shall not touche them. We shall not morne, nor weepe moche for them, for they be in peace and reste. Their soulles be gone to the reste of our Lorde, and he is beneficiall unto them. They be allwais in a joyfle hoope and expectation of the laste daye, when Christe shall saye unto them, Come ye the blyssed of my father, enherite ye the kingdome prepared for you, from the begynnynge of the worlde.'

Before leaving this period of history, I am tempted to depart a little from the path I have followed from the outset—namely, of confining the examples of handwritings strictly to those of the English sovereigns, their wives and children—and to present to the reader examples of the penmanship of men whose names are most nearly associated with the Reformation, or particularly with the translation of the Bible into English.

This great work was accomplished in Henry VIII's reign, and was, for England, the most fruitful work done during that season of conflict and turmoil on the side of both civil and religious liberty. But it was done without any help from, and with scant sympathy on the part of Henry or his bishops—until at any rate the latter part of his reign, when the Bible having been both translated and printed in English, they had begun to perceive the power this weapon put into their hands in the conflict with Rome. Had it been left for king and bishops to initiate the work, as Cranmer said afterwards in his famous letter, it would have been done 'a day after doomsday.' But it *was* done, and mainly by men who were willing to suffer, and, if need be, to die in order that their fellow-countrymen might be able to read the Bible in their mother-tongue. The man manifestly raised up by God for this great work was William Tindale. He translated and printed the English New Testament, partly at Cologne and partly at Worms, in 1525; and in 1534 he printed at Antwerp his revised edition. He had previously at Marburg in Hesse, in 1530, printed the Pentateuch. In 1535 Miles Coverdale issued his Folio Bible. In 1536 Tindale was martyred at Vilvorde, near Brussels; and in 1537 John Rogers, who also under Queen Mary was martyred, printed and published what is known as Matthew's Bible. This large folio, the true primary version of the English Bible, made up of all Tindale's translations and supplemented in the other portions from Coverdale, actually received the king's sanction, although, at the time it was published, all Tindale's writings were under the ban. In 1538, Coverdale, with Thomas Cromwell's co-operation and powerful influence, revised the 1537 Bible, and published in 1539, through Richard Grafton, what was known as the Great Bible. Of this, in two years, six other editions were published, with a Preface by Cranmer, then Archbishop of Canterbury, and hence popularly known as Cranmer's Bible.

Unfortunately it is not possible to get genuine autographs of all the men concerned in this important series of events. We give, however, in the accompanying plate, the only signature of Tindale known, also those of Stephen Vaughan—the ambassador who tried, it is needless to say unsuccessfully, to persuade Henry VIII to believe in Tindale and take him into favour,—of Cranmer, as Archbishop of Canterbury, of Cromwell, of Latimer, as Bishop of Worcester, of Coverdale, and of Richard Grafton. The last two, though affixed to an important contemporary document, were in all probability written by the scribe who penned the letter to Cromwell in which they occur.

Of Henry's half dozen wives, we have examples of the handwriting of five—Catherine of Aragon, Anne Boleyn, Jane Seymour, Anne of Cleves, and Catherine Parr. I do not know of a specimen of Catherine Howard's writing, though no doubt some are in existence.

The following signature of Queen Catherine of Aragon—'Your loving mother Katherina the Qwene'—is appended to a letter[1] written in a clerk's hand from Woburn, probably in the year 1525, to her daughter the Princess Mary, afterwards Queen. In this the writer alludes to the pleasure she feels at her child's study and 'writing in Lattine' being superintended by so able a master of the language as 'Maister Federston.'

[1] British Museum, Cotton MSS., Vesp. F. xiii. f. 72.

EXAMPLES OF PENMANSHIP OF MEN CONNECTED WITH THE EARLY TRANSLATION OF THE BIBLE.

TINDALE.

LATIMER.

CRANMER.

COVERDALE and GRAFTON.

VAUGHAN.

CROMWELL.

Of Anne Boleyn's writing we get a better example. Here is a holograph letter[1] of hers, written to Cardinal Wolsey some three or four years before her marriage to Henry, when she was about twenty years of age. The allusions to her correspondent's efforts to assist her in becoming the king's consort, and her promise of future gratitude, are exceedingly curious, as showing the action taken by the cardinal with regard to Henry's second marriage. The expression, 'how wretched and unworthy I am in comparying to his hyghnes,' is probably an allusion to the position which she held as maid to Henry's first wife. The letter is as follows :—

'My Lord after my most humble recommendacions this shall be to gyve unto your grace as I am most bownd my humble thankes for the gret payn and travell that your grace doth take in stewydeng by your wysdome and gret dylygens howe to brynge to pass honerably the gretyst welth that is possyble to come to any creatour lyvyng, and in especyall remembryng howe wretcchyd and unworthy I am in comparying to his hyghnes. And for you I do knowe my self never to have deservyd by my desertes so that you shuld take this gret payn for me yet dayly of your goodnes I do perceyve by all my frendes and though that I hade nott knowlege by them the dayly proffe of your dedes doth declare your words and wrytynge towards me to be trewe nowe good my Lord your dyscressyon may consyder as yet howe lytle it is in my power to recompence you but all onely with my good wyl the whiche I assewer you that after this matter is brought to pas, you shall fynd me, as I am bownd in the meane tym, to owe you my servyce, and then, looke what thyng in this woreld I can inmagen to do you pleasor in, you shall fynd me the gladdyst woman in the woreld to do yt and next unto the Kynges grace of one thyng I make you full promes to be assewryd to have yt and that is my harty love unfaynydly deweryng my lyf and beyng fully determynd with Goddes grace never to change thys porpos I make an end of thys my reude and trewe meanyd letter, praynyg ower Lord to send you moche increse of honer with long lyfe. Wrytten with the hand of her that besychys your grace to except this letter as prosydyng from one that is most bound to be

'Your humble and
'Obedyent servaunt
'ANNE BOLEYN.'

[1] Holograph. British Museum, Cotton MSS., Vesp. F. xiii. f. 73.

My lord after my most humble recommendacions this shall be to gyve unto yor grace
as I am most bownd my humble thanks for the gret payn and travell that yor
grace doth take in studyeng by yor wysdome and gret dylygent how to bryng
to pas honerably the gretyst welth that is possyble to cum to any creatur lyvyng
and in especyall remembryng how wretchyd and unworthy I am in comparyng
to his highnes / and for you I do knoo my self never to have deservyd by my deserts
that you shuld take this gret payn for me yet dayly of yor goodnes I do perseyve
by all my frends and though that I had nott knowleyge by them the dayly
profe of yor dede doth declare yor wordes and wryttyng toward me to be
trwe now good my lord yor discressyon may consyder as yet how lytle it
is in my power to recompence you but all onely wt my good wyll the whiche
I assuer you that after this matter is brought to pas you shall fynd me
as I am bownd in the mean tyme to owe you my servyse and then look
what thyng in this wordld I can imagyn to do you plesur in you
shall fynd me the gladdyst woman in the wordld to do yt and next
unto the kynges grace of one thyng I make you full promes to be assuryd
to have yt and that is my harty love unfaynydly duryng my lyf
and beyng fully determynyd wt godds grace never to change thys
porpos I make and end of thys my rude and trewe menyng letter
prayng our lord to send you moche increse of honor wt long lyf
wryttn wt the hand of her that besecheys yor grace to acept this letter
as pecedyng from one that is most bownd to be

From Mrs Anne Bullen befor hir Mariadg to the King:

yor humble and
obedient servant
Anne Boleyn

FACSIMILE OF THE HANDWRITING OF ANNE BOLEYN

XI. Henry the Eighth and his Wives

In 1536 Henry procured the execution of Anne Boleyn, and married—three days after her execution—Jane Seymour. Their married life was but of short duration, as she died in the October following, twelve days after the birth of their first child, afterwards Edward VI. A good specimen of her signature exists in a formal letter written at Hampton Court, four months before her death, to the keeper of the royal park at Havering-at-Bower, in which she directs him to furnish 'the gentlemen of the Chapell Royall of my soverayn Lorde the King' with two bucks 'of this season.' The signature reads—'Jane the Quene.'

Henry married Anne of Cleves on January 6, 1540, and was divorced from her a few months later. The 'happy insensibility of temper'—as Hume calls it—which allowed her to consent to live apart from the king, to be to him 'as a sister,' and to accept £3,000 a year 'pension[1],' is shown in the following letter, which she wrote to her step-daughter, the Princess Mary (shortly after the latter's marriage with Philip of Spain), from her country house at Hever, in Kent:—

> *Holograph. Original at the Public Record Office. State Papers, Domestic, Mary. See facsimile on page 67.*

'After my humble commendations unto your Ma^ty, with like thanks for your approved Gentilnes, and Lawful favour shewed unto me in my last sute, praying your Highness of your Loving Continuance, It may please your Highness to understand that I am informed of your Graces return to London again being desirous to do my duty to your Ma^ty, and the King, if it may so stande with your Highness's pleasure. And that I may knowe when and where I shal wayt uppon your Ma^ty and his; wishing you both much joy and felicity, with increase of Children to God's Glory, and to the preservacon of your prosperous Estates long to continue wth honor in all godly Vertue, from my poore house of Hever the 4th of August.

'Your highnes to commande,
'ANNA the daughter of Cleves.

Addressed—'To the Queens Ma^ty.'

[1] She died at Chelsea in 1557.

Taking Henry's wives in order of date, we now come to Catherine Howard, whom he married on July 26, 1540, and who was beheaded on February 12, 1542. As I said previously, I have failed to discover a specimen of her writing, and so will pass on to that monarch's sixth and last spouse, Catherine Parr, whom he married in July, 1543, and who survived him; though, according to the story told by Fox, she had on one occasion a narrow escape of parting with her head. However, there can be no doubt that of Catherine Parr's ability Henry ultimately entertained an opinion very different from that which he had of any of his previous wives, as the facsimile at the side—which shows us Catherine's signature as queen-regent—demonstrates. In the document to which this signature is appended, the queen pleads on behalf of one of her servants that he may benefit from some confiscated church lands: it has many points of interest, though, not being holograph, is unworthy of quotation or representation in the present series. It belongs to the year 1544, when Henry had crossed the Channel to assist the Emperor Charles in his wars against the King of France.

I must not omit to give an example of Henry VIII's signature produced by a 'stamp.' Lingard has referred to the use of this 'stamp,' as if it was necessitated by the king's old age and fatness: but this is not so. We have seen that the idea of such a 'plaything' occurred to the royal mind more than a century before (*ante*, p. 30), and there is no doubt that Henry VIII used to sign a vast number of documents by this means from quite the early days of his reign.

Stamp used by Henry VIII in the early part of his reign.

Stamp on the King's Will: see p. 69.

What happened in his old age was this. He became so stout and so infirm that the mere process of impressing this 'stamp' on the document became

FACSIMILE OF THE HANDWRITING OF ANNE OF CLEVES.

XI. Henry the Eighth and his Wives

irksome, and then he gave formal authority to three 'Commissioners' to use it for him; and in this singular manner :—two impressed the 'stamp,' dry, on the document, and then the third, with a penfull of ink, filled in the outlines of the letters left by the dry stamp. For safety's sake the commissioners had to furnish the king, at the end of each month, with a list of the documents they had thus signed, and some of these lists are still extant. An actual instance of the signature so produced occurs on Henry VIII's will, and the validity of that instrument has been questioned on that account.

XII

EDWARD VI

HENRY VIII was the last English sovereign who could truthfully plead bad penmanship as an excuse for being a bad correspondent. After the Reformation, elegance in handwriting was no longer aimed at alone by persons ecclesiastical; it became a fashionable study amongst the laity, and the fruits of the fashion are shown very plainly in the caligraphy of Henry VIII's children—Edward VI, Mary, and Elizabeth, and in that of Lady Jane Grey.

Edward VI has left us two interesting specimens of his early compositions—one in Latin (*facsimile*, p. 71), the other in French (*facsimile*, p. 72), and both characteristic of his fondness of study—addressed to his mother.

Turning from these boyish effusions, we come to a letter which—though its exact meaning is veiled—may have had, and indeed probably had, considerable political importance. Edward is no longer prince, but king, and in that capacity he addresses the Senate of Zurich in terms of the warmest cordiality, hailing them as cemented to him in friendship by the similarity of their religious belief. This friendship, he says, 'by God's blessing' shall be yet firmer than it is, and for that purpose he sends his messenger to lay before them, 'in our name,' some other things 'which we have thought fit should, at this time, be made known to you.' There was but one subject on which Edward was likely to have special reason for communicating with Zurich, and that subject was

XII. Edward the Sixth

religion—the spread and the permanent establishment of Protestantism. Little doubt, therefore, that the communications with which the English messenger was charged, related to this, and would—could it be known—be of deep interest to the student of Reformation history.

> Fortasse miraberis me tā sepe ad te scribere, idq̄ tā breui tempore, Regina Nobilissima, & Mater Charissima, sed eadem ratione potes mirarj me erga te officium facere. Hoc autem nunc facio libentius, quia est mihi idoneu nuncius seruus meus, & ideo non potuj non dare ad te literas ad testificandū studiū meū erga te. Optime valeas Regina Nobilissima. Hunsdome, Vigesimo Quarto Maij.
>
> Tibj obsequentissimus filius.
> Edouardus Princeps.
>
> Illustrissimæ Reginæ
> Matri meæ.

The letter, now preserved amongst the State Archives of Zurich, is signed at the head by the king, and is written by a clerk. It is a beautiful example of the careful penmanship of the time, and certainly an appropriate illustration to this volume [1]. (*See facsimile* facing page 73.)

---

[1] For furnishing us with a photograph of this letter, we are indebted to the kindness of M. Labhart-Labhart—the Archivist at Zurich.

Handwriting of the Kings and Queens of England

FACSIMILE OF A LETTER FROM PRINCE EDWARD TO HIS MOTHER.

Je vous mercie tresnoble & tresexcellente Roine de voz lettres lesquelles vous menvoiastes dernierement non seulement pour la beaute de voz lettres mais aussy pour linuention des mesmes lettres. Car quand ie voiois vostre belle escriture & lexcellence de vostre engin grandement precedant mon inuention ie nauois vous escrire. Mais quand ie pensois que vostre nature estoit si bonne, que toute chose procedant dun bon esprit et vouloir si acceptable, ie vous ay escrit ceste lettre cy. De ma maison de Hampton court.

Edward.

In translation the letter reads thus:—

'Edward the Sixth, by the grace of God, of England, France, and Ireland, King, Defender of the Faith, and of the Church of England and Ireland, supreme head upon earth, &c. To the honourable and valiant Lords of Zurich, our right entirely beloved friends, greeting. After we had taken upon ourselves, by ancient and hereditary right, the government of our kingdoms, nothing was more ardently desired by us than to conciliate, and most firmly retain, the friendship of those sovereigns who had been especially esteemed by our most serene father of most happy memory: and, as in the number of these he always regarded, as long as he lived, your most noble and valiant nation, so

LETTER FROM EDWARD VI. SIGNED BY THE KING AT THE END.

XII. Edward the Sixth

we likewise cannot but regard you with especial esteem, and exceedingly value your friendship; and the rather, because we have understood by the frequent letters of our faithful and beloved servant, Christopher Mont, both your favourable disposition towards us, and ready inclination to deserve well of us. In addition to which, there is also a mutual agreement between us concerning the Christian religion and true godliness, which ought to render this friendship of ours, by God's blessing, yet more intimate. We therefore return you our warmest thanks for your singular and favourable disposition towards us, which you shall always find to be reciprocal on our part, whenever an opportunity shall present itself. We have therefore commanded this our servant to salute you most cordially, to inform you more fully of our affection and good-will, and to lay before you, in our name, some other things which we have thought fit should, at this time, be made known to you. We therefore earnestly request you to place assured and undoubting reliance upon what he shall communicate. So farewell. From our palace at Westminster, Oct. 20, A. D. 1549, and of our reign the third.

'Your good friend
'(Signed) EDWARD.'

A little more than two months after the date at which was written the letter to Zurich, we have that from the king to the bishops, in which he enjoins the use of the Book of Common Prayer throughout the land. Although the fact of this letter having been written may be notorious history, yet its importance as an item in the working out of the Reformation in England, renders it of special interest to the readers of these pages, and also worthy of facsimile. Besides the signature of the king, it also furnishes examples of those of Cranmer, Warwick, and other prominent men who then formed the Council. The letter reads as follows :—

Original at British Museum, Stowe MSS. 155. *See facsimile on pages 76 and 77.*

'EDWARD.

'By the King.

'Right reverend father in god, right trustie and welbiloued, we grete you well. And whereas the booke entiteled the booke of common prayers and administracion of the sacraments and other rightes and ceremonies of the church after the vse of the churche of England was agreed vpon and sette forth by acte of parliament and by the same acte commaunded to be vsed of all personnes within this our realme, yet neuertheles we ar enfourmed that divers vnquiet and evell disposed personnes syns the apprehension of the Duke of Somerset haue noysed and bruted abrode that they shulde haue agayne their olde Laten seruice their conjoured breade and water with such like vayne and supersticious ceremonies; as though the setting forth of the said booke had been the onelye acte of the aforenamed Duke. We therfore by the aduise of the bodye and state of our Privie Counsell not onelie considering the said booke to be our owne acte and thacte of the whole state of our realme, assembled together in parliament, but also the same to be grounded vpon holye scripture, agreable to the ordre of the primatiue church and muche to the edifieng of our subiectes to put away all such vayne expectacion of having the publike seruice the administracion of the sacramentes and other rightes and ceremonies agayne in the Laten tong which were but a preferring of ignorance to knowledg and darkenes to light and a preparacion to bring in papistrie and supersticion agayne—haue thought good by thaduise aforesaid to require and neuerthelesse straytlie commaund and chardg you that ye immediately vpon the receipt herof do commaund the Deane and prebendaries of your Cathedrall church the parson, viccar or curate and churchwardens of every parishe within your diocesses to bring and deliuer to you or your deputie [and] every of them for their church and parishe at suche convenient place as ye shall appoynte all antyphoners, missalles, grayles, processionalles, manuelles legendes pyes portases journalles and ordynalles after the vse of Sarum, lyncoln, Yorke, Bangour, Hereford or any other pryvate vse and all other bookes of seruice, the keping wherof shuld be a lette to the vsing of the said booke of common prayers and that ye take the same bookes into your handes or into the handes of your deputie and them so deface and abolish that they never herafter maye maye (*sic*) serve either to any suche vse as they wer first provided for, or be at any tyme a lette to that godlye and vniforme order which by a common consent is now set forth. And if ye shall fynd any personne stoubbourne or disobedient in not bringing in the said bookes according

FACSIMILE OF A LETTER FROM EDWARD VI AND

THE COUNCIL TO THE BISHOPS, *vide pp.* 73-79.

XI. Edward the Sixth 79

to the tenure of theis our letters, that then you commyt the same person to warde to suche tyme as ye haue certified vs of his misbehaviour, and we woll and commaund you that ye also serche or cause serch to be made from tyme to tyme whether any bookes be withdrawne or hydde contrary to the tenure of theis our letters, and the same bookes to receyve into your handes and to vse as in this our letters we haue appoynted. And furthermore wheras it is comme to our knowledg that dyvers froward and obstynate personnes do refuse to paye towardes the fynding of breade and wyne for the holye communion, according to the ordre prescribed in the said booke by reason wherof the holye communion is many tymes omitted vpon the sondaye. Theis ar to will and commaund you to convent such obstinate personnes before you, and them to admonish and commaund to kepe thordre prescribed in the said booke, and if any shall refuse so to do, to punishe them by suspencion excommunicacion or other censours of the churche. Fayle ye not thus to do as ye will avoyd our displeasure. Geven vnder our signet at our palace of Westminster the xxv[th] of December the third yere of our reign. [A. D. 1549.]

'T. Cant.   R. Ryche Canc.   W. Seint John.
H. Dorssett.   J. Russell.
Arundell.   Thomas Elien.   J. Warwyk.'

Somerset, it will be remembered, had been arrested in the same month as that in which the letter to Zurich had been written, so that his signature does not occur amongst those of the Council in the letter to the bishops. The Protector's position in the State, however, entitles his signature to a representation here, and we therefore give a facsimile of it, taken from a curious warrant to dispose of surplus stock from the royal wardrobe, dated (after his restoration to favour with the king) in December, 1550.

The other example of his handwriting is furnished by some verses from Scripture written by him on the fly-leaf of a volume containing the Calendar, a Table of Moveable Feasts, and the like. The quotations have additional interest from the fact that they were penned by the Protector on the eve of his execution.

fere of the lord
is the boenning of
his dinme
put thi trust in
the lord w all
thine hart
be not wise in thine
owne consexte but
fere the lord and
fle frome enele
frome the towere
the day before
1551
E. Somerset

XI. Edward the Sixth

to the tenure of theis our letters, that then you commyt the same person to warde to suche tyme as ye haue certified vs of his misbehaviour, and we woll and commaund you that ye also serche or cause serch to be made from tyme to tyme whether any bookes be withdrawne or hydde contrary to the tenure of theis our letters, and the same bookes to receyve into your handes and to vse as in this our letters we haue appoynted. And furthermore wheras it is comme to our knowledg that dyvers froward and obstynate personnes do refuse to paye towardes the fynding of breade and wyne for the holye communion, according to the ordre prescribed in the said booke by reason wherof the holye communion is many tymes omitted vpon the sondaye. Theis ar to will and commaund you to convent such obstinate personnes before you, and them to admonish and commaund to kepe thordre prescribed in the said booke, and if any shall refuse so to do, to punishe them by suspencion excommunicacion or other censours of the churche. Fayle ye not thus to do as ye will avoyd our displeasure. Geven vnder our signet at our palace of Westminster the xxv[th] of December the third yere of our reign. [A. D. 1549.]

    'T. CANT.   R. RYCHE CANC.   W. SEINT JOHN.
    H. DORSSETT.   J. RUSSELL.
    ARUNDELL.   THOMAS ELIEN.   J. WARWYK.'

Somerset, it will be remembered, had been arrested in the same month as that in which the letter to Zurich had been written, so that his signature does not occur amongst those of the Council in the letter to the bishops. The Protector's position in the State, however, entitles his signature to a representation here, and we therefore give a facsimile of it, taken from a curious warrant to dispose of surplus stock from the royal wardrobe, dated (after his restoration to favour with the king) in December, 1550.

E: Somerset

The other example of his handwriting is furnished by some verses from Scripture written by him on the fly-leaf of a volume containing the Calendar, a Table of Moveable Feasts, and the like. The quotations have additional interest from the fact that they were penned by the Protector on the eve of his execution.

> fere of the lord
> is the beginning of
> wisdume
> put thi trust in
> the lord is all
> thine hart
> be not wise in thine
> owne conseyte but
> fere the lord and
> fle frome evele
> frome the towere
> the day before
> 1551
> E Somerset

XIII

'JANE THE QUEEN' AND PHILIP AND MARY

APART from the personal interest which attaches to the handwriting of the unhappy 'nine days' Queen,' the fact that Lady Jane Grey signed, as Queen, certain official documents, is a reason for including her name in the present papers and giving specimens of her writing. Before, however, alluding to examples of her writing, after her ill-advised assumption of the title of Queen, I will refer to a letter written by her at the age of eleven; its composition is characteristic of her learning, and the genuine tone of gratitude which pervades it, of her unaffected disposition. The letter is addressed by the writer to her uncle, the Lord High Admiral Seymour.

Original at Public Record Office. State Papers, Domestic, Edward VI. Vol. V, No. 5. Holograph. Facsimile on page 83.

'My dutye to youre lordeshippe in moste humble wyse remembred, withe no lesse thankes for the gentylle letters whiche I receavyd from you, Thynkynge myselfe so muche bounde to youre lordshippe for youre greate goodnes towardes me from tyme to tyme that I cannenot by anye meanes be able to recompence the leaste parte thereof. I purposed to wryght a fewe rude lines unto youre lordeshippe rather as a token to shewe howe muche worthyer I thynke youre lordshippe's goodnes then to gyve worthye thankes for the same and thes my letters shall be to testyfye unto you that lyke as you have becom towardes me a lovynge and kynd father so I shall be always most redye to obey youre godlye monytyons and good instructions as becomethe one uppon whom you have heaped so manye benyfytes. And thus fearynge leste I shoulde trouble youre lordshippe to muche, I moste humblye take my leave of your good lordeshippe.

'Youre humble servant durynge my lyfe,

'JANE GRAYE.'

Addressed—'To the right honorable and my essingular good Lorde, the Lorde Admiralle, yeve this.'

Lady Jane assumed the title of Queen on the 6th of July, 1553. Amongst the Privy Seals for that year is one of the few public instruments which she executed. It directs a patent to be prepared for the appointment of Edward Baynard [or Bénardé, as she spells his name], Esq., as Sheriff of Wilts, in the room of a deceased sheriff. The appointment by 'Queen' Jane is dated on the 14th of July, eight days after the death of Edward VI. It will be noticed that the sheriff's name is inserted by Jane in her own handwriting.

Translation. Original at the Public Record Office. Facsimile opposite.

'JANE THE QUENE.

'Let letters patent be made, appointing Edward Bénardé sheriff of the county of Wilts in the room of Sir William Sharington, knight, deceased, late sheriff of the county aforesaid.

'Witness—14th day of July.'

Attached to the slip of parchment which bears this appointment is another slip inscribed as follows:—

Translation.

'MARYE THE QUENE.

'Let letters patent be made appointing Edward Baynarde sheriff of the

My dutye to youre lordshippe in moste humble wyse remembred withe no lyke thankes for the pe
lettrs whiche I receauyd from you Thynkynge my selfe so muche bounde to youre lordshippe for
greate goodnes towardes me from tyme to tyme that I cannot by anye meanes be able to ren
the laste parte thereof. I purposed to wryght a fewe rude lines unto youre lordeshippe rathe
token to shewe howe muche worthyer I thynke youre lordshyppes goodnes then to gyve worti
thankes for the same and this my letters shall be to testyfye unto you that lyke as you have
towardes me a louynge and kynd father so I shall be alwayes moste redye to obey youre god
mysyons and good instructions as becometh one uppon whom you have heaped so ma
benyfytes and thus feurynge leste I shoulde trouble youre lordshyppe to muche I moste hu
take my leaue of your good lordeshippe.

            youre humble seruant
            my lyfe Jane graye

JANE the Quene

Auant &c. damus ad constituend Edwarde Benarde
...

Ðe xvj die July

XIII. 'Jane the Queen' and Philip and Mary

county of Wilts in the room of Sir William Sharington, knight, deceased, late sheriff of the county as aforesaid.

> 'Be it remembered that on the 6th day of July in the 1st year of the reign of Queen Mary this Bill, &c., at Framlingham for execution.'

It should be noticed that Mary's appointment is not dated, and it is probable that it was drawn up and signed by the queen on the very day of her accession, and sent at once to the chancellor for execution, the day of its

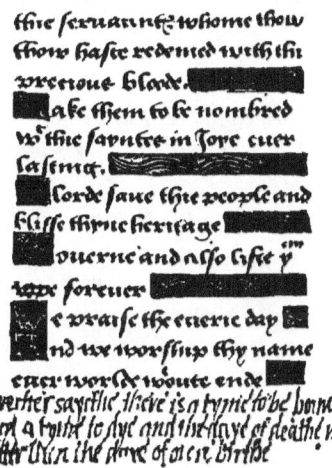

receipt in Chancery being the actual day of Edward VI's death—the 6th of July. But the subsequent turn of events may have put Edward Baynard in some little doubt as to what step to take to ensure the possession of the shrievalty; and to make all things certain, smooth, and straight he probably obtained from Jane an appointment, of which no formal notice was ever taken by the Chancery officials. This is probably the correct story of these two intensely interesting slips of parchment.

But perhaps the relic of Lady Jane Grey which awakens the most romantic interest is the small manual of prayers, two pages of which are figured above.

The writing at the foot of each page is that of the unhappy lady, and the manual is believed to have been that used by her upon the scaffold.

The hostility of Devonshire to the altered form of service—which, as we have seen, was enjoined in 1549—is demonstrated by the outbreak early in the following year, in which the populace clamoured for the restitution of the Mass, and that respect should be shown to holy water and holy bread. We are not, therefore, surprised to find—in the interesting letter from the new queen to some of her justices of the county in question—that on her accession her proposed alliance with Philip of Spain, and the restoration of the Roman Catholic religion, were heartily welcomed at least by a section of Devonshire people. Here is the letter which bears Mary's signature at its head:—

Original at the Public Record Office. State Papers, Domestic, Mary. Vol. II, No. 5. Facsimile of one page is given opposite.

'By the Quene.

'MARYE THE QUENE.

'Trusty and welbiloved, we grete you well. And where certain lewd and ill disposed persons minding to set furth their devilish sedicious purposes, sum to the hinderaunce of the true Catholicq religion and divine service, now by the goodness of God restored within this our realm, other of a traitorous conspiracy against our personne and state royall, have of late, and still do maliciously publishe, many false rumours of the cumming of the high and mighty prince our deerest cousin the Prince of Spayne, and others of that nation into this our realm. Albeit we nothing doubt but all our good loving subgetes of the honnest sort have that affiance of us, that we neither have, nor will, during our lief agree to any thing that may be to the hinderaunce or prejudice of thauncient libertes, fredoms, and communwelth of this our realm or subgetes; yet to satisfie such as through the crafty malice of other be perchaunce abused with this thing, we have caused the very true effect of tharticles of the treatye, lately concluded, to be delivred to sundry persons of credit, to be by them published in sundry partes of our realm, wherewith as we do right well knowe, the great part of our subgetes be (as they have good cause) right well satisfied. So being credibly enformed that the great nombre of our good subgetes of that our county of Devon have shewed themselves

LETTER TO COUNTY JUSTICES SHOWING QUEEN MARY'S SIGNATURE AT THE HEAD.

By the Quene

Marye the quene

Trusty and welbelovid we grete you well. And whereas certain lewd and ill disposed persons, minding to set furthe their devillyssh pretensed purposes, sum to the hinderaunce of the true catholyq religion and divine servyce now by the goodnes of god restored within this our realm, other of a traitorouse conspyracy agaynst our persone and state royall. Sum of late and still do malicyouslye publisshe many false rumours of the cumming of the most mighty prince our derest cousyn the prince of Spayne and others of that nacion in to this our realm. Albeit we nothing doubt but all our good loving subjects of the goodest sort have that affiaunce in us that we neither have nor will during our lyfe assent to any thing that may be to the hinderaunce or preiudice of thauncient liberties fredome and common weele of this our realm or subjects; yet to satisfye sum and thorough the crafty malice of others be perhaps abused in this thing; we have caused the very some and effect of theffecte of the treatye lately concluded to be reduced to sundry persons of credit, to be by them publisshed in sundry partes of our Realme / wherefore, as we do right well knowe, the great part of our

XIII. 'Jane the Queen' and Philip and Mary

well willing to obey and serve us, notwithstanding sum lewd practises of late unnaturally attempted, and many false and untrue reportes spred amonges them, we have thought good to signifie unto you, by these our letters, that we take and accept the same in very thankfull part, and shall not faile to have it in our good remembraunce. Which our good determination towards them, our pleasour is, ye shall cause to be published unto them, so as the good, being thereby the better comforted to contynue in their duetyes of allegeaunce, may take the better hede and beware of thauthors of thies, or any such like false bruts and rumours. Whereby as they shall best provide for their own suretes, quiet, and preservation, so shall we not faile to see them succoured and provided for, and be glad to shew ourselvelfes their good and gratious Lady as often as any occasion may serve. Geven under our signet at our Manour of St James the 22nd of January the furst yere of our reign.'

Addressed—

'Our trusty and welbeloved Sr Hugh Pollard, Sr John St Leger, Sr Richard Edgecombe, Sr John Fulford, Knightes & every of them.'

Mary married Philip in July, 1554. The following example of the signatures of the king and queen appears on an appointment of certain persons to the care and management of the royal revenue, dated April 12, 1555.

Yet one more specimen of Mary's handwriting may be appropriately given It appears, in Latinized form, attached to a document which relates to a very curious circumstance in her history, namely, the hallucination under which she laboured during a portion of the first year of her married life, that she was about to give birth to a child. How strongly this delusion impressed her, and how generally she convinced those around her of the truth of her conjectures, is shown by this extremely interesting letter (written in May, 1555), which, with only the date left blank, was intended to convey to Pope Paul IV the joyful news of the birth of an heir to the English crown born of Catholic parents.

Original in the British Museum, Cotton MSS., Vesp. F. 3, No. 23. Translation.

'To the most holy father our Lord, Pope Paul IV, by divine providence Chief Pontiff, Mary, by the grace of God, Queen of England, France, Naples, Jerusalem, Ireland, &c. Eternal Greeting and our most humble obedience. We are so strongly assured of your paternal love and affection for us as to think that no happiness can befall us without affording your holiness singular gladness as well. Therefore we consider that nothing more behoves us than that we should first signify to your holiness that God has, at this time, blessed us by a labour as easy to ourself as propitious to our subjects, and has in his marvellous goodness towards us given unto us the child we so much wished for. We therefore desire your holiness that in like manner as your holiness will rejoice at this our sure happiness, so you will, with us, offer up your pious prayer to God for the benefit thus vouchsafed unto us. May God long have your holiness in his Holy keeping. From our place of Hampton ——— 1555.

Addressed—
'To the most holyfather our Lord Pope Paul the IVth by divine providence chief pontiff.'

In translation 'Your holiness' most humble daughter, MARY,' the word 'Maria' only is written by the Queen.

XIV

ELIZABETH

MOST of us know Queen Bess as a good penwoman. Like her brother and sister, she evidently received a very careful training in handwriting. Edward VI's early death has prevented us from learning what fruit this tuition would have borne in after-life; in Mary's case her writing—as we have seen—became slightly more slovenly as she advanced in years; but Elizabeth wrote a firm clear hand almost to the day of her death.

Here is a letter which may, with interest, be compared with the early compositions of her brother, sister, and Lady Jane Grey; Elizabeth was fourteen when she wrote it. The letter—which belongs to the year 1547—is addressed to the Queen Dowager, Catherine Parr, and illustrates the affectionate relations that had all along existed between Henry's child by Anne Boleyn and his widow. It reads as follows:—

Holograph. Original at Public Record Office. State Papers, Domestic, Edward VI. Vol. II, No. 25. See facsimile on p. 93.

'Althougth I coulde not be plentiful in givinge thankes for the manifolde kindenis receyved at your hithnis hande at my departure, yet I am some thinge to be borne with al, for truly I was replete with sorowe to departe from your highnis, especially levinge you undoubful of helthe, and albeit I answered litel, I wayed it more dipper whan you sayd you wolde warne me of al evelles that you shulde hire of me, for if your grace had not a good opinion of me you wolde not have offered frindeship to me that way, that al men iuge the contrarye, but what may I more say than thanke God for providinge suche frendes to me, desiringe God to enriche me with ther longe life, and me grace

Handwriting of the Kings and Queens of England

to be in hart no les thankeful to receyve it, than I nowe am glad in writinge to shewe it. And althougth I have plentye of matter, hire I wil staye, for I knowe you ar not quiet to rede. Frome Cheston this present Saterday.

'Your hithnis humble doughter

'ELIZABETH.'

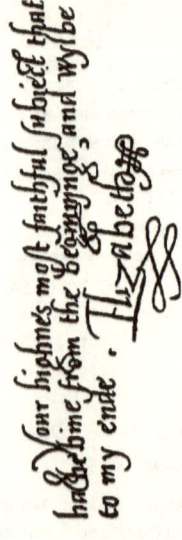

Seven years after the date of this letter, Elizabeth, whose profession of Protestantism caused her sister continual uneasiness, was committed to the Tower under the pretext of complicity in Sir Thomas Wyatt's rebellion. Though lying seriously ill in Hertfordshire at the time of her arrest, she was carried with but scant ceremony to London and kept as a prisoner at Whitehall. On the Friday before Palm Sunday, 1554, the Bishop of Winchester and nineteen members of the Council entered her presence, formally charged her with being concerned with Wyatt, and acquainted her with her sister's order that she should be lodged in the Tower. Thither she was accordingly removed on Palm Sunday, permission having been first given her to write a letter to the queen. This letter, perhaps one of the most interesting in many ways that Elizabeth ever wrote, is too long for either quotation in full or for facsimile reproduction in its entirety, but some account of it, and a representation of its concluding words, must find a place in these pages[1].

'I humbly crave but only one worde
of answer fro[m] your selfe.

'Your highnes most faithful subiect that hathe
bine from the begininge, and wylbe
to my ende.
'ELIZABETH.'

---
[1] Holograph. Original at Public Record Office. State Papers, Domestic, Mary, vol. iv, No. 2.

FACSIMILE OF A LETTER FROM QUEEN ELIZABETH TO CATHERINE PARR.

Although I coulde not be plentiful in giuinge thankes for the manifolde kindenes receyued at your hithnis hande at my departure, yet I am some thinge to be borne with al, for truly I was replete with sorowe to departe frome your highnis, especially leuinge you vndoubful of helthe, and albeit I answered litel I wayed it more dipper whan you sayd you wolde warne me of al euelles that you shulde hire of me, for if your grace had not a good opinion of me you wolde not haue offered frindeship to me that way, that al men iuge the contrarye, but what may I more say than thanke God for prouidinge suche frendes to me, desiringe God to enriche me with ther longe life, and me grace to be in hart no les thankeful to receyue it, than I nowe am glad in writinge to shewe it. and although I haue plentye of matter, hire I wil stay, for I knowe you ar not quiet to rede. Frome Cheston this present saterday.

Your hithnis humble doughter
Elizabeth

XIV. Elizabeth

'If,' begins the Princess, 'any ever did try this olde saynge that a Kinges worde was more than another mans othe, I most humbly beseche your Majestie to verefie it in me and remember your last promise and my last demande that I be not condemned without answer and due proof; which it seems that now I am.' The Tower, she thinks, is a place 'more wonted for a false traitor than a tru subject,' and sending her thither will condemn her in the eyes of the world, though God knows her to be innocent of any machinations against her sister. 'Therefore,' she continues, 'I humbly beseche your Majestie to let me ansver afore your selfe and not suffer me to trust your counselors; yea, and that afore I go to the Tower, if it be possible; if not, afor I be further condemned.' However it may be, she trusts that no evil report brought to Mary will, without full investigation, set 'one sistar again the other,' and then again protesting her freedom from complicity with the 'traitor Wiat,' she proceeds: 'I pray God confound me eternally if ever I sent him word, message, token, or lettar by any menes, and to this my truith, I wil stande in to my dethe.'

It is needless here to dwell upon the stimulus which Protestantism received by the accession of Elizabeth. The numerous foreigners professing the Reformed religion who by 1558 had become denizens of England had good cause to hail her accession to the English throne with something akin to enthusiasm. During her sister's rule the Dutch Protestant settlers in London, to whom Edward VI had given the church of Austin Friars, were forced to dissolve their congregation; its numbers, no doubt, to a large extent, returned to the Continent, and the church was given to the Marquis of Winchester. Now came the joyful tidings that a Protestant sovereign once more reigned over England, one who, as the minute-books of the Dutch congregation express it, 'greatly favoured the Reformation, to the rejoicing of all true Christians.' But from various fragments of evidence preserved to us it seems that, a little later on, these worthy foreigners were not quite satisfied with the terms on which they obtained a restoration of their church. Their elders had, on the reassembling of the Congregation, petitioned the Privy Council for a confirmation of the free and unrestricted grant they had formerly received from Edward VI. What they got we see by the following, which is addressed to the Marquis of Winchester; and which, as it bears Elizabeth's signature, is an appropriate document for special facsimile [1].

[1] See plate facing next page.

Original at the Public Record Office. State Papers, Domestic, Elizabeth.
Vol. XI, No. 24.

'ELIZABETH R.

'By the Quene.'

'Right trusty and right welbeloved cousin we grete you well. Whereas in the tyme of our brother, and suster also, the churche of the late Augustyn Frears was appointed to the use of all strangers repayring to the cittie of London for to have therein dyvine service. Consideringe that by an universall order, all the reste of the churches have the dyvine service in the englisshe tonge, for the better edefieinge of the people, which the strang[er]s borne understand not. Our pleasure is that ye shall assigne and delyv[er] the said churche and all thing[es] thereto belonging to the Reverend father in God, the busshopp of London to be appointed to suche curate and mynisters as he shall thinke good to serve from tyme to tyme in the same churches bothe for daily Divine servyce and for administra[ti]on of the Sacraments, and preaching of the gospell. So that no right nor use be therein observed contrary or derogatory to o[u]r lawes. And theis our l[ette]res shalbe yo[u]r sufficient warrant and discharg[e] in that behalf. Yeven under o[u]r signet at o[u]r palace of Westm[inster] the —— of February, the seconde yere of o[u]r Reigne.'

The letter is endorsed—'The Queene to yᵉ Tresorer Powlett yᵉ 2d off her Raynge.'

This is a very material document in the history of the foreign Protestants in England, and indeed in the history of the Church of England. Elizabeth will be no party to those frequenting a foreign church having any form of service they might fancy. Austin Friars is therefore given, not to the elders of the congregation, but to the Bishop of London, who—though he might permit divine service to be in the language of the foreigners—was to see that it was celebrated daily, and in the form of the Church of England: this, I think, is the interpretation which must be given to the words, 'so that no right nor use be therein [i.e. in the church] observed contrary or derogatory to o[u]r lawes.' How far the queen's order was observed is not a matter which we need dwell upon here. Mr. W. J. C. Moens gives a capital sketch of the

LETTER FROM QUEEN ELIZABETH SIGNED AT THE HEAD

XIV. Elizabeth

history of the Congregation in his 'historical introduction' to the Registers of the church which he printed, privately, in 1884.

The two following facsimiles give us examples of Elizabeth's signature as queen, at the commencement and close of her reign. The first[1] is

appended to a document dated in August, 1561, addressed to the Receiver-General of the Court of Wards and Liveries, giving him direction as to

passing his accounts. The second signature[2] is appended to a document bearing date in February, 1602, by which the queen directs Admiral Sir

---

[1] Public Record Office. State Papers, Domestic, Elizabeth, Addenda, vol. xi, No. 25.
[2] Ibid., vol. cclxxxiii, No. 28.

Richard Leveson to sail from Plymouth in The Repulse, with nine ships, and intercept the fleet that was believed to have been despatched from Spain to effect a landing in Ireland.

Amongst the State Papers[1] is a letter from the Earl of Leicester to Elizabeth, written about a week before his death, which happened on September 4, 1588. The letter itself has no particular feature of interest; the writer inquires after the queen's health, 'the chiefest thing in this world' he prays for, and he speaks hopefully of his own speedy recovery; but the endorsement, in Elizabeth's own hand, has a very special interest; it reads as follows :—

'To ye Q[ueen's] most excellent Ma[jes]t[ie] *his last letter*'; the words in italics are in Elizabeth's writing.

The strength of the testimony borne by this endorsement to the regard which the queen then entertained for Leicester, will best be understood when we remember her habit of banishing from memory those who had passed away from her presence. How the letter found its way into the public papers of the kingdom we do not know, but there can be no doubt that at first the queen preserved it as the last letter she received from a former suitor for her hand.

Our last specimen of Elizabeth's writing is a prayer, believed to have been composed for the safety of the ships which she despatched in 1597 to scatter the Spanish fleet preparing to attack Ireland. On their way to Spain the English vessels were dispersed by a storm, and the commander, the Earl of Essex, confined his efforts to intercepting the Spanish ships on their way to the Indies.

---

[1] Public Record Office. State Papers, Domestic, Elizabeth. Addenda, vol. ccxv, No. 65.

PRAYER COMPOSED BY QUEEN ELIZABETH.

O god all-maker, keeper, and guider: Inurement of thy rare-seene, vnused and seeld-heard-of goodnes, powred in so plentifull sort vpon vs full oft, breeds now this boldnes, to craue with bowed knees, and heartes of humilitye, thy large hande of helping power, to assist with wonder ouro iust cause, not founded on Prides-motion nor begun on Malice-stock. But as thou best knowest, to whome naught is hid, gratified on iust defence from wronges, hate, and bloody desire of conquest: For since meanes thou hast imparted to saue that thou hast giuen, by enioyng such a people, as scornes their bloodshed, where suretie ours is one: Fortifie (Deare God) such hartes in such sort, as their best part may be worst, that to the truest part meant worst, with least loste to such a Nation, as despise their liues for their Cuntryes good. That all-Forrine Landes may laud and admire the Omnipotency of thy worke: A fatt alone for thee only to performe. So shall thy name be spread for wonders wrought: And the faithfull encouraged, to refuse in thy Vnfellowed grace: And wee that minded naught but right, inflamed in thy boundes, for perpetuall slauery, and saie and sye the Sacrifices of oure soules for such obayned fauoure. Warrant (Deare Lorde,) all this with thy command.

Amen.

XIV. Elizabeth

Holograph. Original at British Museum. Harl. MSS. 6986, *No.* 35.
See facsimile opposite.

'O God all-maker, keeper, and guider: Inurement of thy rare-seene, unused and seeld-heard-of goodnes, powred in so plentifull sort upon us full oft, breeds now this boldnes to crave with bowed knees, and heartes of humilitye, thy large hande of helping power, to assist with wonder, oure iust cause, not founded on Prides-motion nor begun on Malice-stock; But as thou best knowest, to whome nought is hid, grounded on just defence from wronges' hate, and bloody desire of conquest. For scince, meanes thou hast imparted to save that thou hast given, by enjoyng such a people, as scornes their bloodshed, where suretie ours is one: Fortifie (deare God) such heartes in such sort, as their best part may be worst, that to the truest part meant worst with least losse to such a Nation, as despise their levst for their Cuntryes good. That all Forreine Landes may laud and admire the Omnipotency of thy worke: a fact alone for thee only to performe. So shall thy name be spread for wonders wrought, and the faithfull encouraged, to repose in thy unfellowed grace: And wee, that mynded nought but right, inchained in thy bondes for perpetuall slavery, and live and dye the sacrificers of oure soules for such obtayned favoure. Warrant, (deare Lorde) all this with thy command. Amen.'

XV

JAMES I AND ANNE OF DENMARK

THE handwriting of James I suggests that the science of caligraphy was not considered a requisite feature in the royal education in Scotland. His writing lacks character, and contrasts very unfavourably with that of his immediate predecessors on the English throne. A noticeable feature in all his writing is the spelling, which is decidedly 'Scotch.'

We know with what eager interest both Protestants and Catholics watched the accession of James I to the throne of England; each party regarded the event with suspicion. The former were indeed not slow to give outward expression to their fears of the 'papistical' tendencies of the new monarch. And it was this fact that drew from James a 'Declaration' which forms an interesting item in the religious history of England.

The form taken by the Declaration was that of a letter addressed by the king to the bishops. This, or rather the draft of it, is preserved amongst the State Papers, and bears marks of having been very carefully revised by James himself, so that a facsimile of a portion of it may appropriately be introduced here. The portion I have selected is the fourth page of the draft; but as this does not show us the commencement of the sentence, I have, in the following transcript, thought better to give some words from the previous page, and some from the next : the interlineations, which are printed in italics, show the king's handwriting.

DRAFT OF A LETTER TO THE BISHOPS CORRECTED BY JAMES I.

XV. James the First and Anne of Denmark

Draft, corrected by the King. Original at the Public Record Office. State Papers, Domestic, James I, Vol. XII, No. 87*.

'We resolved for our discharge to God and towards all men first to make a publick declaration to our whoale counsayle in the presence of our Archbishopp of Canterbury with divers other Bishopps how much we tooke it to hart that all thinges should be duly performed which might tend to the preservation of that trew religion wherein we have ever lived and resolve to dye. We did likewise cause the Recorder of London to be sent for, to yeild us an accompt what had been done ^ *either by vertu of our comandment* concerninge the apprehension of Priests ^ [*by vertue of our own commandm^t and by perticuler*¹] *and such as use to repaire either publickly or privatly to heare mass, or by such perticuler* dyrections [*receaved from*] *as* our counsayle ^ *had given him to the same end,* from whom receavinge less satisfaction then we expected ^ *especially* consideringe the [*circumstances of the*] *strange* reports delivered unto us ^ *of those great scandales which our good subjects receaved by such insolent abuses* [*of publick goinge to masses in the citty*], we commanded him to impart unto the Maior and other officers how much we misliked that any [*remissnes*] *coldnes* should be used, commandinge them uppon their duty and allegeaunce not only to be carefull to trye out and apprehend all persons whatsoever soe offendinge by their owne authoritye, but allsoe to be diligent uppon all occasions to informe our privye counsayle of such enormitys, to the intent that whensoever there shall be cause to make use of further authoritye then their owne ordinarye power, their proceedings may be strengthined with that extraordinary authoritye which we doe leave with them at all tymes for matters of so great consequence.'

It would be difficult to give a more interesting specimen of James's penmanship than that afforded by the sixteen interrogatories which he prepared for the guidance of the Commissioners appointed to examine Guy Fawkes in reference to the famous Gunpowder Plot. First, says 'the wisest fool in Christendom,' let the Commissioners inquire 'quhat he is, for I can never yett here any man that knowis him;' and then he sets out more than a dozen other questions to be put to the prisoner as to his past life, including the inquiry 'if he was ever a papiste; and if so, quho brocht him up in it.' If he will answer these questions willingly, well and good; but, adds the

¹ The words enclosed in brackets are struck out by James.

king, 'if he will not confesse, the gentler tortours are to be first used unto him, *et sic per gradus ad ima tenditur*, and—so God speede your good worke— JAMES R.'[1] (*See facsimile at the side.*)

We get, however, a better idea of James's powers of composition in the following letter, by which he desires his son, Charles Prince of Wales, to return home quickly from Spain, whither he had gone to seek the hand of the Infanta. The visit, we remember, was taken chiefly at the instigation of Buckingham, who, by his arrogant behaviour at the Spanish Court, soon disgusted those he presumably desired to please. James, it seems, had got wind of how matters stood at Madrid, and was consequently anxious to get both his son and Buckingham home ere matters became more complicated. The letter reads as follows :—

Holograph. Original at British Museum. Harl. MSS. 6987, *f.* 143. *Facsimile opposite.*

'My dearest sonne, I sent you a comandement long agoe not to loose tyme quhaire ye are; but ather to bring quikelie hoame youre mistresse, quhiche is my earnist desyre; but if no bettir maye be, rather then to linger any longer thaire, to come without her, quhiche for manie important reasons I ame now forcid to renew. And thairfor I charge you upon my blessing, to come quikelie ather with her or without her. I knowe youre love to her person hath enforcid you to delaye the putting in execution of my former comandement. I confesse it is my cheifest wordlie ioye, that ye

[1] Original at Public Record Office. Gunpowder Plot Papers.

LETTER OF JAMES I TO HIS SON CHARLES, PRINCE OF WALES

My dearest sonne, I sent you a comandement long agoe
not to loose tyme quhaire ye are, but aither to bring
quitelie hoame youre mistresse, quhiche is my
earnist desyre, but if no bettir maye be, rather
then to linger any longer thaire, to come without
her, quhiche for manie importante reasons I ame
now forcid to renew, & thairfor I charge you upon
my blessing, to come quitelie aither with her or without
her, I knowe youre loue to her person hath enforcid
you to delaye the putting in execution of my forme
comandement, I confesse it is my cheifest wordlie
ioye, that ye loue her, but the necessitie of my affaires
enforcith me to tell you, that ye muste preferre the
obedience to a father to the loue ye carrie to a
mistresse & so god blesse you.
James R

Coornburne the 10 of auguste.

XV. James the First and Anne of Denmark

love her, but the necessitie of my effaires enforcith me to tell you, that ye muste praeferre the obedience to a father to the love ye carrie to a mistresse. And so God blesse you.

'JAMES R.

'Cranburne the 10 of Auguste [1623].'

Of the handwriting of Anne of Denmark we get many examples. The following letter—addressed to Buckingham—is characteristic, and points

> My kind dog, I haue receaued y^r your letter which is verye well=com to me yow doe verie well in Lugging the sowes eare, and I thank yow for it, and would haue yow doe so still vpon con=dition that yow Continue a watchfull dog to him and be alwaies true to him, So wishing you all happines
>
> Anna R.

to the terms of familiarity on which the favourite lived with the royal family. Its date must be between August, 1616, when Buckingham was created Viscount Villiers, and the January following, when he was created Earl of Buckingham:—

Holograph. Original at British Museum. Harl. MSS. 6986, No. 109. See facsimile on previous page.

'My kind dog, I have receaved your letter, which is verye wellcom to me: yow doe verie well in lugging the sowes eare, and I thank yow for it, and would have you doe so still, upon condition that yow continue a watchfull dog to him and be alwaies true to him. So wishing you all happines

'ANNA R.'

Addressed—'To the Viscount Villiers.'

XVI

CHARLES I AND HENRIETTA MARIA, HENRY PRINCE OF WALES, AND ELIZABETH QUEEN OF BOHEMIA

THE specimens left to us of the handwriting of Charles I during his boyhood show that his education in penmanship was better than that which we may presume his father received. In the several letters of Charles I, written before he was twelve years old, extant amongst the Harleian MSS., we see a writing formed with considerable skill, bearing even favourable comparison with the early efforts of Edward VI. In after years, Charles wrote an exceedingly well-formed hand—the first really good 'running' hand which we meet with among the handwritings of our English sovereigns.

Here is a letter signed by Charles, and evidently composed by himself, in which he expresses his willingness to part with all his worldly possessions in return for his brother Henry's love.

Original at British Museum. Harl. MSS. 6986, No. 85.

'Sweet, Sweet Brother, I thank you for your letter. I will keip it better then all my graith, and I will send my pistolles by Maister Newton, I will give anie thing that I have to you, both my horse, and my books, and my peices, and my crosse bowes, or anie thing that you would haive. Good Brother, loove me and I shall ever loove and serve you.

'Your looving brother to be comanded,

'YORK.'

Another letter, written by Charles to his brother Henry, probably a year or so after the foregoing, shows us the former's powers of Latin composition.

Holograph. Original in Latin at the British Museum. Harl. MSS. 6986, No. 90. Facsimile opposite. Translation.

'Nothing can be more pleasing to me, most dear brother, than your return to us; for to take pleasure with you, to ride with you, to hunt with you, will be the highest gratification to me. I now read the colloquies of Erasmus, from which I am confident that I shall be able to learn purity of the Latin language and elegance of style. Farewell.

'Your most loving brother,

'CHARLES DUKE OF ALBANY AND YORK.'

The object of thus writing was, that Henry might judge how the writer was progressing in his schooling, a matter in which he was evidently deeply concerned. This fact is in itself noteworthy, for it must be remembered that Prince Henry was then barely in his 'teens'—surely an early age for a boy to be anxious as to the progress of a younger brother's education? But Henry had an extraordinary craving for knowledge, the capacity which his father had, or thought he had, for obtaining it, and also a desire that others should taste the fruits of learning. He also had, as we have seen by his brother's previous letter, the power common to all the Stuarts, except his father, of engaging the love of those around him. We

FACSIMILE OF A LATIN LETTER WRITTEN BY CHARLES TO HIS BROTHER HENRY.

Nihil possit mihi esse gratius, Frater charissime, tuo ad nos reditu; te enim frui, tecum equitare, tecum venari, summæ erit mihi voluptati. Ego iam lego Erasmi colloquia, ex quibus et Latinæ linguæ puritatem et morum elegantiam discere posse me, confido. Vale.

Tuæ Cels.ⁿⁱˢ frater amantissimus

Carolus Eb. et
Alb. Dux

XVI. Charles the First and his Family

know, too, that Henry had another gift—tact; a gift to which certainly all the later members of his family were strangers. For that reason, alone, his early death was probably the greatest misfortune that ever befell the House of Stuart. Space precludes us from giving more than an example either of Prince Henry's signature [1], or of that of Elizabeth [2], his sister, who became Queen of Bohemia.

[signatures]

We will now turn to some examples of Charles's handwriting after his accession.

In the early summer of 1627 the Duke of Buckingham sailed on his memorable—and, in its termination, disastrous—expedition to the Isle of Rhé in order to relieve the besieged Huguenots. The scarcity of money and provisions with which the expedition was furnished, soon made itself felt, and Buckingham despatched Sir William Beecher home, to urge that supplies be forthwith sent out. The state of Charles's finances at this period of history is well known, and he sought to increase the revenue by the levy of excessive duties on imports and exports. The proposal was opposed as unconstitutional by the ministers, and so the king's impatience was aroused. The

[1] Original in British Museum. Cotton MSS., Vesp. F. iii, f. 11 b.
[2] Original at Public Record Office. State Papers, Domestic, Charles I, vol. ccxxxvi, No. 44.

following is the last of three letters written by him to the Exchequer officers, and its wording leaves us in little doubt as to the frame of mind of the writer.

Holograph. Original at Public Record Office. State Papers, Domestic, Charles I. Vol. LXXIII, No. 1. The facsimile shows the first five lines.

'Tresorers

'Now I begin to see sum good effects of your labors, yet, it is but a begingin, and if ye goe not speedelie on to make an good end (I meane of those things that ar to be spedd out of hand) all that is past, is worthe littell or nothing: By the next, and verrie shortlie too, I looke to heare, that those things I sent Beecher to you about, ar dispached; For if Buckingham should not now, be suplyed, not in show, but substantiallie, having so bravelie, and, I thanke God, succesfullie, begunne his expedition, it wer an irrecoverable shame to me, and all this Nation; and those that ether hinders, or, according to ther severall places, furthers not this action, as much as they may, deserves to make ther end at Tyburne, or some suche place: But I hope better things of you. I lykewaise looke for an accont of the Mint business, and of the raysing of my Costomes; I hope ye will be industrius in all my affairs, but in this of the Costomes, I looke ye should add bouldness to your care. So expecting a full and perfect account of all those things that I have earnestlie recommended to you, at Windsor if not sooner; I rest

'Your asseured frende

'CHARLES R.

'Woodstock the 1 of August, 1627.'

Addressed—'For your selves.'

I. Portion of Prayer written by Charles I.

Good Lord I thanke for keeping mee this day, I humble beseche thee to keepe mee this night from all dangers or mischances that may happen to my Boddie, Grant evell thoughts which may goads- or hurt my Sand. for Jesus Christ his sake: And looke upon me thy unworthie servant, who heere prostrates him selfe at thy throne of grace, but looke upon mee

II. Draft of Letter to Queen Henrietta Maria.

Deare harte, by Sadrans conveyance (whom I dispached Sonday last) I hope thou wilt receave 3 leaers from me; who although before as can gone to thee. he condemes the Rebelles proceedings as much as any, yet he declares in his Maisters name a positive Neutrality, so that ether he employes not with his Instructions, of France is not so much our frend as we hope for.

XVI. Charles the First and his Family

In odd contrast to the arbitrary demand for worldly help is the following prayer for the aid of heaven, written by the king some five years later, and, by a choice of readings, made suitable for morning or evening use. It seems to be compiled partly from the Book of Common Prayer, and partly from the Bible.

Holograph. Original at Public Record Office. State Papers, Domestic, Charles I. Vol. CCXI, No. 91. The facsimile shows the first four and part of fifth lines.

'Good Lord I thanke [Thee] for keeping mee this $\frac{day}{night}$, I humblie beseeche Thee to keepe mee this $\frac{night}{day}$ from all dangers or mischances that may happen to my Boddie, and all evell thoughts which may assalt or hurt my Sowel, for Jesus Christ his sake : And looke upon me Thy unworthie servant, who heere prostrates him selfe at Thy Throne of grace, but looke upon mee O Father through the merites and mediation of Jesus Christ Thy beloved Sone, in whom Thou art onlie well pleased, for of my selfe, I am not worthie to stand in Thy presence, or to speake with my uncleane lips, to Thee, most holly and æternall God; for Thou knowest that in sinn, I was conceaved and borne, and that ever since I have lived in iniquetie, so that I have broken all Thy Holly Commandments, by sinfull motions, evell words and wicked workes, ommitting manie dewties I ought to doe, and committing manie vyces, which Thou hast forbidden under paine of heavie displeasure: as for sinnes, O Lord, they ar innumerable in the multitude. Therefore of Thy mercies, and by the merites of Jesus Christ, I intreate Thy Devyne Majestie that Thou wouldest not enter into jugement, with Thy servant; nor bee extreame to marke what is done amisse, but bee Thou mercifull to mee, and washe away all my sinnes, with the pretius [blood] that Jesus Christ shed for me : and not onlie washe away all my sinnes, but also to purge my hart, by [Thy] Holly Spirit, from the drosse of my naturall corruption ; and as Thou doest add dayes to my lyfe, so (good Lord) add repentance to my dayes, that when I have past this mortall lyfe, I may bee a partaker of Thy everlasting Kingdome, throught Jesus Christ our Lorde.'

Handwriting of the Kings and Queens of England

During the progress of the Civil War, Charles was an active correspondent. To his wife he wrote frequently, and generally in hopeful tones, even if circumstances, for the time, looked unpropitious. Here is a specimen—the draft of a letter written probably from Oxford in January, 1645. Henrietta Maria was then in France, whither she had fled during the previous summer in order to escape possible danger. The king's advice to his wife as to her policy towards the Queen Regent of France is interesting.

Holograph. Original at Public Record Office. State Papers, Domestic, Charles I. See facsimile on p. 118, which shows the first six lines.

' Deare hart

'I hope before this can come to thee, thou wilt receave 3 letters from me by Sabran's conveyance (whom I dispached Sonday last); who although he condemes the Rebelles proceedings as much as any, yet he declares, in his Maisters name, a posititive newtrality, so that ether he complyes not with his Instructions, or France is not so much our frend as we hope for. I rather thinke the later: yet I dout not but thy dexterity will cure that couldness of frendship, which, in my opinion, will be the easier done, if thou make the cheefe treaty for our assistance betwixt thee and the Q. R.[1] in a familliar obliging way: and withall showing all possible respect and trust to those Ministers whom she most esteemes; it being impossible, but they must rather aplaude, then dislyke, thy familiarity with theire Mistris, and by it, thou may prevent any trickes they may put upon thee. As for the affaires heere, wee are in so good state, that I am confident the Rebelles (though all their strenthes ar now united) cannot afront us, and when my nepueu Rupert comes to mee (whom I certainly expect in few dayes) I hope to be able to choose freshe Winter quarters, but where, I am not yet resolved, for which occasion and oportunitie must direct mee.'

The majority of letters now extant written by Henrietta Maria are in French; the following, in English, introduces us to an amusing incident in the history of Charles II's boyhood.

[1] The Queen Regent.

LETTER FROM QUEEN HENRIETTA MARIA TO HER SON.

charles j am sore that j most begin my
forst letter with chiding you be
cause j heere that you will not take
phisike j hope it was onlei for this
day and that to morrow you will
doe it for if you will not j
most come to you and make
you take it for it is for your healthe
j haue giuen order to mylord neucastell
to send mi worde to night whether
you will or not therfore j hope you
will not giue mi the paines to goe
end so j rest
your affectionate mother
HENRIETTE MARIE

XVI. Charles the First and his Family

Holograph. Original at British Museum. Harl. MSS. 6988, *No.* 25.
See facsimile opposite.

'Charles, I am sore that I most begin my first letter with chiding you be cause I heere that you will not take phisike. I hope it was onlie for this day, and that to morrowe you will doe it, for yf you will not, I most come to you and make you take it, for it is for your healthe. I have given order to my lord Newcastell to send mi worde, to night, whether you will or not, therfore I hope you will not give mi the paines to goe, end so I rest

'Your affectionat moher [*sic*]

'HENRIETTE MARIE R.'

XVII

OLIVER AND RICHARD CROMWELL

THE following letter from Oliver Cromwell, written to his wife from Edinburgh on April 12, 1651, though not of political importance, gives us an insight to the Protector's domestic style. The pious ejaculations with which it abounds are certainly characteristic of the man who wrote it. Cromwell married in 1620 a daughter of Sir James Bourchier, a gentleman who owned considerable landed property in Essex. 'Bettie,' alluded to in the letter, was his favourite daughter, Elizabeth Claypole.

Holograph. Original at British Museum. Egerton MSS. 2620, fol. 9.
See facsimile opposite.

' My Deerest,

'I praise the Lord I am encreased in strength in my outward man, but that will not satisfie mee, except I gett a heart to love and serve my heavenly Father better, and gett more of the light of his countenance, wch is better then life, and more power over my corruptions, in theise hopes I waite, and am not without expectation of a graicious returne. Pray for mee, truly I doe daylie for thee, and the deere family, and God Almighty blesse you all with his spirituall blessinges. Minde poore Bettie of the Lords late great mercye, oh I desire her not only to seeke the Lord in her necessitye, but indeed and in truth to turne to the Lord, and to keep closse to him, and to take heede of a departinge heart and of beinge consu[m]ed with worldly vanityes, and worldly companie, wch I doubt shee is too subject to. I earnestly, and frequently pray for her, and him, truly they are deere to mee, very deere, and I am in feare least Sathan should

Letter from Oliver Cromwell to his Wife.

My Dearest /

I praise the Lord I am encreased in strength in my outward man, but that will not satisfie mee, except I gett a heart to love and serve my heavenly Father better, and gett more of the light of his countenance, wch is better then life, and more power over my corruptions, in theise hopes I waite, and am not without expecta- tion of a gracious returne, pray for mee, truly I doe daylie for thee, and the deere family, and God Almighty blesse you all with his Spirituall blessings. mynde poore Bettie of the Lords late great mercye, oh I desire her not only to seeke the Lord in her necessity, but indeed and in truth to turne to the Lord, and to keepe close to him, and to take heede of a departinge heart, and of beinge cousend with worldly vanityes, and worldly companie, wch I doubt shee is too subiect to. I earnestly, and frequently pray for her, and him, truly they are deere to mee, very deere, and I am in feare least Sathan should deceave them, knowinge how weake our hearts are, and how subtil the adversarie is, and what way the deceitfullness of our heartes, and the vaine world make for his tentations: the Lord give them truely of heart to him, lett them seeke him in truely and they shall finde him. my love to the deere little ones, I pray for grace for them, I thanke them for their letters, lett mee have them often.

Truely I am not able as yett to write much, I am weary, and rest, thine, Oliver Cromwell

Thou doest not write to mee whiles thou tarryest att Hampton-Court, but I hope I shall shortly see thee. I rest, thine, I beseech thee to have a care of my dearest, and the pretty little ones, I pray for grace for them. I have committed thee, and them, to the Lord. Bidd Betty be serious, the Lord looke upon her. I pray for her, and tell her from mee, I hope shee is willing to submitt to the Lord. I pray for her often, and truly I am not able as yett to write much, I am weary, and rest, thine.

April the 12th 1651.

XVII. Oliver and Richard Cromwell

deceave them, knowinge how weake our hearts are, and how subtill the adversarie is, and what way the deceiptfullnesse of our heartes, and the vaine world make for his tentations; the Lord give them truth of heart to him, lett them seeke him in truth and they shall finde him. My love to the deere little ones. I pray for grace for them. I thanke them for their letters, lett mee have them often. Beware of my Lord Harbert, his resort to your house (if hee doe soe) may occasion scandall, as if I were bargainnge with him, indeed bee wise, you know my meaninge. Minde Sr Hen. Vane of the businesse of my estate, wch indeed is very tickle (*sic*), as Mr Floyde can enforme you. I know hee beares a freindes minde, Mr Floyd knowes my whole minde in this matter. If Dick Cromwell and his wife bee with you, my deere love to them, I pray for them they shall (God willinge) shortly heere from mee, I love them very deerly, truly I am not able as yett to write much, I am wearye, and rest

'Thine

'O. CROMWELL.

'Aprill the 12th 1651.'

Addressed—

'For my beloved Wife, Elizabeth Cromwell att the Cockpitt these.'

We give also below a bolder specimen of his signature :—

As Richard Cromwell was nominally Protector for a few months after the death of his father, a specimen of his writing ought perhaps to appear here. The following letter, which bears his signature, addressed to his former friend, General Monck, is in many ways an interesting one, since we gather from it an accurate picture of the straitened circumstances in which he was placed within a month of this declaration of Breda.

Original at British Museum.   Egerton MSS. 2618, fol. 67.

'My Lord,

'Allthough I cannot suppose you altogether unacquainted with my present condition, nor insensible of what my friends have represented to you concerning it, yet being urged by my present exigencies & necessitated for some time of late to retire into hiding-places to avoid arrests for debts contracted upon the publiq account, I have been incouraged, from the perswasion I have had of yor affection to mee, and the opportunitie you now have to show mee kindnesse, to add this request to the former solicitations of my friends, that, when the Parliament shall bee met, you would make use of yor interest on my behalfe, that I bee not left liable to debts which I am confident neither God, nor conscience, can ever reckon mine. I cannot but promise myselfe that when it shall bee seasonable, I shall not want a faithfull friend in you to take effectuall care of my concernements: having this perswasion of you that as I cannot but thinke myselfe unworthy of great things, so you will not thinke mee worthy of utter ruine.

'My Lord, I am,

'Your affectionate friend to serve you,

R Cromwell

'Aprill 18, 1660.'

Addressed—'For his Excellencie the Lord Generall Monck these.'

Endorsed—'Apr. 1660. Lord Rich. Cromwell for security from debts.'

XVIII

CHARLES II AND CATHERINE OF BRAGANZA

THERE can be no doubt that Charles II never liked the triple alliance which England, Holland, and Sweden entered into in 1668. By it, these three countries compelled France to yield to their demands; and, as it was to France that Charles chiefly looked for aid in casting off the tiresomely constitutional yoke of Parliament, he took the earliest opportunity of concluding a secret treaty with France which nullified the effects of the distasteful alliance. The secret treaty was signed at Dover in 1670. The next move was, of course, to pick a quarrel with Holland, and the best means of doing this was to replace Temple, a popular ambassador at the Hague, by Sir George Downing, a particularly odious one to the Dutch. However, the following very interesting letter shows us that even Downing did not act sufficiently promptly in bringing matters to a crisis. The want of proper respect to the British flag was, we see, to be the avowed basis of the quarrel.

Holograph. Original at British Museum. Stow MSS. 458. See facsimile on page 131, showing concluding paragraph of the letter.

'Whithall, Jan. 16, [O. S.] 167$\frac{1}{2}$.

'Sr George Downing, I have seene all your letters to my Ld Arlington, since your arrivall in Holland; and because I finde you sometimes devided in your opinion betwixt what seemes good to you for my affaires in the various emergencyes and appearances there, and what my instructions direct you, that you my not erre in the future, I have thoughte fitt to send you my last minde upon the hinge of your whole negotiation, and in my owne hand, that you may likewise know it is your part to obey punctually my orders, instead of putting yourself to the trouble of finding reasons why you do not do so, as I find in your last of the 12th currant. And first you must know I am entierly secure that France will joine with me against Holland, and not seperate from me for any offers Holland can make to them. Next I do allow of your transmitting to me the States' answer to your memoriall concerning the flag, and that you stay there expecting my last resolution upon it, declaring that you cannot proceede to any new matter till you receave it; but upon the whole matter you must always knowe my minde and resolution is not only to insist upon the haveing my flag saluted, even on there very shoare (as it was alwaies practised), but in haveing my dominion of these seas asserted, and Wan Guert exemplarily punished.' Notwithstanding all this, I would have you use your skill so to amuse them, that they may not finally dispaire of me and therby give me time to make myselfe more ready and leave them more remisse in these preparations.

'In the last place I must againe injoine you to spare no cost in informing your selfe exactly how ready there ships of warre are, in all there ports, how soone they are like to put to sea, and to send what you learne of this kinde hether with all speede. I am

'Your loveing frend,

'CHARLES R.'

(*See facsimile on opposite page.*)

The whole letter is thoroughly typical of Charles II's character, and it is only lack of space that prevents a full facsimile being given. Two months later, on March 17, 1672, England and France declared war upon Holland, during which some of De Ruyter's greatest sea-battles were fought.

I have not met with a specimen of the handwriting of Charles II's queen, Catherine of Braganza, in English; there are, however, some interesting letters in Portuguese written from Lisbon before the future queen's arrival in England. The signature on the opposite page is appended to one, written to Charles, in which she prays God to send 'your Majesty's servant, the fleet,' to her with speed and safety, that she may the sooner accomplish her

XVIII. Charles the Second and Catherine of Braganza

journey to England. She speaks of the happiness which 'those kingdoms of yours, which your Majesty is pleased should also be mine,' must feel at the restoration of their 'lawful king[1].'

[In translation.]
'Your Majesty's most faithful wife, who kisses your hands,

Sua mui fiel melher q suas maós beija

'CATHERINA R.'

PORTION OF LETTER FROM CHARLES II TO SIR GEORGE DOWNING.

In the last place I must againe inioine you to spare no cost in informeing your selfe exactly how ready these ships of warre are in all these ports, how soone they are like to put to sea, and to send what you learne of this kinde hether with all speede, I am

Your loveing frend

Charles R

[1] Original at Public Record Office. State Papers. Portugal. Sept. 3, 1661.

XIX

JAMES II, ANNE HYDE, MARY OF MODENA, AND THE LATER STUARTS

JAMES II, both as Duke of York and as King, was a very prolific writer. His handwriting is bold, and suggests the work of a man possessed of a firmer character than his enemies, or even his friends, will allow that he possessed. I have selected as a specimen of his handwriting, a letter written by him in August, 1685, to the Prince of Orange. His allusions to the magistrates of Amsterdam who had taken the part of the Duke of Monmouth in the recent rebellion, show that William either intended, or pretended that it was his intention, to punish any partisans of Monmouth whose complicity could be demonstrated. James's allusions to the military display at Hounslow are interesting, especially that to the mounted Grenadiers.

Holograph. Original at British Museum. Additional MSS. 28,103, *fol.* 68.
See facsimile on pp. 134-5.

'Windsor Aug: 25 : 1685.

' I have receved yours of the 27: by which I am very glad to find, you do agree, to what I proposed to you, concerning the E : of Pembrook, and thanke you very kindly for doing it, and shall send to advertise him of it, that he may make what hast he can over to you to thanke you for your kindnesse to him. As for the names of any of the Magistrats of Amsterdam, when I can gett any authentike proffs against them, I shall lett you have it, w[ch] I feare will be hard to be gott, tho tis certaine some of them knew of the D : of Mon : designe. On Saturday last I saw some of my troops at Houndslow, they consisted of ten

LETTER OF JAMES II TO THE PRINCE OF ORANGE.

Windsor Aug: 25: 1685.

I have receued yours of the 27: by
which I am very glad to find, you
do agree, to what I proposed to you,
concerning the E: of Pembrook, and
thanke you very kindly for
doing it, and shall send to aduertise
him of it, that he may make what
hast he can ouer to you to thanke
you for your kindnesse to him, as for
the names of any of the Magistrats
of Amsterdam when I can gett any
authentike proofs agaienst them
I shall lett you haue it, w:ch I feare
will be hard to be gott, tho 'tis
certaine some of them knew of
the D: of Mon: designe, on saturday

last I saw some of my troupes at Houndslow, they consisted of ten Battallions of foot, of w:ch three were of the gards, and the other seven new raised Reg:ts of horse, there was twenty Squadrons, and one of granaders on horse back and one of Dragoons, and realy the new troupes of both sorts, were in very good order, and the horse very well mounted, I was glad that the Mareschal d'Humieres saw them, for severall reasons, I have not tyme to say more now but that you shall always find me as kind to you as you can desire.g.

XIX. James the Second, his Wives, and the later Stuarts

Battallions of foott, of wch three were of the gards, and the other seven new raised Reg^a; of horse, there was twenty squadrons, and one of granaders on horse back, and one of Dragoons, and realy the new troups of both sorts, were in very good order, and the horse very well mounted. I was glad that the Mareschal d'Humieres saw them, for severall reasons. I have not tyme to say more now but that you shall always find me as kind to you as you can desire. J.'

Addressed—' For my sonne the Prince of Orange.'

As in this instance the king signs only his initial, we give below a copy of his signature in full.

James married his first wife, Anne Hyde, daughter of the famous Earl of Clarendon, very shortly after the Restoration. She was possessed of but slight beauty, but of very brilliant powers of conversation. The marriage—which had been contracted secretly—was for some time regarded with disfavour by the royal family; and the Earl of Clarendon himself, though probably well pleased at an event which would bring him more closely in contact with the king, expressed surprise and even disgust at the extravagance of his daughter's pretensions. The whole affair and what followed reflects little credit on any of those concerned in it. At the time that Anne wrote the letter—the signature to which we give below—all had been lived down, and she was received at Court with the respect due to her. She was then with her husband at York, and she tells her sister that it is a ' really good place,' better than Salisbury, which was apparently her former home. Hospitality, enough and to spare, was shown to James and his wife. 'We are like,' she says, ' to have many feasts ; to-morrow my Lord Mayor makes us one, which will be very troublesome!'

Anne died in 1671, having first been received into the Roman Catholic communion, an event which caused considerable popular uneasiness with regard to the religious faith of her husband. About two years later James married Mary Beatrice, daughter of the Duke of Modena, who with her infant son fled to France a few days before her husband's abdication in 1688. The letter below is written from the Stuart Court, at St. Germains, probably at the close of the year 1692, or the commencement of 1693, and addressed to John Caryll—titular Lord Caryll—the faithful adherent of the fugitive royal family.

Holograph. Original at British Museum. Additional MSS. 28,224, folio 2.

'I made bold last night to open these letters of yours, seeing ther were others in it, I took out one for Lady Sophya, and one for Strickland; hear is your owne, which have not been out of my hands. I hope your cough is better, and that it will soon permitt you to com again amongst us. Wee are all well, God be thanked, and my daughter has been weened with greater facility then I could have hoped for.

'M. R.'

XIX. James the Second, his Wives, and the later Stuarts

The daughter referred to was the Princess Louisa Maria, who died unmarried in 1712.

Here we may appropriately give representations of the signatures of the three last male representatives of the House of Stuart—James and Charles (the 'old' and the 'young' pretender, or 'James III' and 'Charles III,' as they are designated, according to taste), and Henry of York, the Cardinal, Charles's younger brother.

James R.   *Charles P.*

Votre Bon Ami
Henry

XX

WILLIAM III AND MARY

IN the specimen which we gave of James II's handwriting, penned in August, 1685, we saw him writing to his son-in-law with an evident absence of anything like suspicion. Whether or not that fearlessness was then well-founded, or at what particular time William of Orange began first to contemplate the invasion of England, are matters which would occupy too much time to discuss. No doubt the birth of James's son in June, 1688, finally resolved him on hazarding the attempt.

William, accompanied by a considerable fleet and some 14,000 men, landed at Torbay from Helvoetsluys on the 5th of November following the date of the prince's birth. The letter from which the extract below is taken is

LETTER FROM QUEEN MARY TO LADY SCARBOROUGH, 1692.

Kensington July ye 29th 90. 12 at night

I always promised Lady Scarburgh to write when there had happen'd any thing the first I asked after when ye news of ye battle came was yr & finding him not mentioned in any of ye letrs tels is for ye best signe for there is an exact acount come so much as of ye Lieutenants of ye part who are either wounded or kild by wch tho you shoud hapen to have no letter yet you may be sure he is well, I thank God ye King is so & tho we have got no victory yet ye French have had an equal losse so yt thay need not brag we have great reason to thank God for thus much & I hope you will sone be well enough to come hither if we may rejoyce together where you will be very welcom to one who will ever be yr affectionate kind friend

MARIE R.

the battle was fought sunday last, from 9. till 6.

XX. William the Third and Mary

written in a firm, bold hand. It is dated 'Au camp de Torbay,' on the day after landing, and is addressed to William's Admiral, Arthur Herbert, afterwards created Earl of Torrington, who tarried behind in Holland. William announces his safe arrival, and intention of marching, without delay, upon Exeter, whither, as shown by the extract, he desires reinforcements from Holland to be sent.

Translation. Original in French. British Museum. Egerton MSS. 2621, *folio* 39. *See facsimile on p.* 140.

'It is necessary that you send the regiments of Hagedorn and Fagel, in one or two small frigates, to the Exmouth River, in order that I may cause them also to come to Exeter.

'I am always yours,

'GUILLAUME PRINCE D'ORANGE.'

Below is William's signature as King of England. It is attached to a warrant dated at the commencement of the year 1689.

Early in 1692 William embarked for Holland to follow up the campaign against the French, which for some time he had been carrying on with but indifferent success. Affairs in England were, during his absence, left in the hands of the queen, who gave evidence of her capacity for government by conducting them with tact and ability. The incidents of the year's campaign were equally unfortunate. At Steinkirk [or Enghein] William was defeated on Sunday, July 24, after nine hours' fight. The news reached the queen at Kensington late on the following Friday, and she hastened to convey to her friend Lady Scarborough, tidings of Lord Scarborough's safety. The letter, which is in the queen's writing throughout, is interesting as giving an account of the defeat as it first reached England, and shows that the writer's mind was prepared for the possibility of a more serious disaster to her husband's forces: 'tho we have got no victory yet ye french have had an equal losse, so y^t thay need not brag.'

Holograph. Original at the British Museum. Additional MSS. 20,731, *folio* 2. *See facsimile on p.* 142.

'Kensington Jully ye 29th 92. Twelve at Night.

'I always promised Lady Scarburgh to write when there had hapen'd any thing. The first I asked after when ye news of ye batle came was y^r L^d and finding him not mentioned in any of ye leters, take it for ye best signe, for there is an exact acount come so much as of ye Lieutenants of y^o Gards who are eithere wounded or kild by wch tho you shoud hapen to have no leter yet you may be sure he is well. I thank God ye King is so, and tho we have got no victory yet ye french have had an equal losse so y^t thay need not brag. We have great reason to thank God for thus much, and I hope you will sone be well enough to come hithere y^t we may rejoyce together where you will be very welcom to one who will ever be y^r afectionate kind friend

'MARIE R.

'The batle was fought Sunday last, from 9 till 6.'

K

LETTER FROM QUEEN ANNE TO THE EARL OF NOTTINGHAM.

Thursday

The enclosed was given me to night, & I have bin soe much desired to save ye womans life, yt I can't help sending it to you to desire you would enquire as soon as it is possible if it is proper to do any thing in it, for to morrow she is to be executed, but if she be one of those yt the Lord did not think a fitt object of mercy, when mr Recorder made his report, I have nothing more to say for her,

I am your very affectionate freind ANNE R

XXI

ANNE AND GEORGE OF DENMARK

HUME tells us that the middle-statured lady, whose effigy now presides at the top of Ludgate Hill, earned for herself the title 'Good' as much from indolence and weak understanding, as from 'any active principle of benevolence.' Be that as it may, in the following letter, written in 1703 to the Earl of Nottingham, we see her bestirring herself in the interests of some poor woman who on the morrow was going to pay the penalty of the law. The queen's appreciation of her Secretary of State's sound judgment is shown in this letter.

Holograph. Original at the British Museum. Additional MSS. 29,548, folio 37. Facsimile opposite.

'Thursday.

'The enclosed was given me to night, and I have bin soe much desired to save ye womans life, y^t I can't help sending it to you to desire you would enquire as soon as it is possible if it is proper to do anything in it, for to morrow she is to be executed, but if she be one of those y^t the Lords did not think a fitt object of mercy, when Mr Recorder made his report, I have nothing more to say for her.

'I am your very affectionett freind

'ANNE R.'

Queen Anne, at the instigation of her uncle, Charles II, married in 1683, George, Prince of Denmark; he died in 1708. His signature is appended[1].

[1] British Museum. Additional MSS. 28,094, fol. 184^d.

XXII

GEORGE I

TO find an interesting letter of such a thoroughly uninteresting character as George I, is, on the face of it, so hopeless that I have not attempted the task. The following is a fair type of his compositions preserved to us. It is addressed to the Emperor Charles V, and was to be carried to him by Abraham Stanian, who was being sent as English ambassador to Constantinople.

Holograph. Translation. Original in French. British Museum. Additional MSS. 22,046, folio 48. Facsimile opposite.

'My Brother! Having found it convenient to order Mr. Stanyan, my envoy extraordinary and plenipotentiary, near you, to return to the Ottoman court as my Ambassador, I have charged him at the same time to reiterate to your Imperial and Catholic Majesty, in the strongest manner, the assurance of my sincere friendship towards you, and how I wish him to render service by that embassy and to make known to Your Imperial and Catholic Majesty more and more that I am most perfectly

'Your Imperial and Catholic Majesty's most affectionate brother

'GEORGE R.

'At Hampton Court
the 17th of October 1717.'

I have not met with a specimen of the handwriting of George I's queen, Sophy Dorothy of Zelle.

LETTER FROM GEORGE I TO THE EMPEROR CHARLES V.

Monsieur mon Frere ayant trouvé apropos d'ordonner au Sieur Staujan mon Envoié extraordinaire & Pleni potentiaire aupres de vous, de se rendre a la Cour Impe riale en qualité de mon ambassadeur, je l'ay chargé en mesme tems de reiterer à Votre Majesté Imperi: & Catholique de la maniere la plus forte, les asseurances de mon amitié sincere envers elle, & combien je sou haitte de luy rendre service par cette ambassade & de faire voir à Votre Majesté Imperiale & Catholique de plus en plus que je suis tres parfaite De Votre Majté Imple & Cathe

Le tres affectionné Frere

George R

à Hampton Cour
le 12 d'Octobre 1727

XXIII

GEORGE II AND WILHELMINA CAROLINA, HIS WIFE

THOUGH Georgè I occasionally spoke English, his accent was atrocious. He seldom trusted himself to write the language of the people he had been called to reign over, whom to the last he regarded as foreigners, and with whose sentiments he was never in touch. George II came to England as a younger man, and entered more into English ways. He spoke and wrote English fairly well; but as he was only a little more interesting a personage than his father, it is almost as useless to seek for an entertaining example of his composition. That below was written in 1759, about a twelvemonth before his death, and is addressed to the Duke of Newcastle, the minister whom he had been forced, two years previously, to recall to office. The letter itself refers to the despatch of a messenger, probably to Germany; but the king's monetary dealings with Newcastle, which the letter mentions, may not be without significance, when we remember it was that minister who dispensed the money which during George II's reign was so lavishly expended in Parliamentary and other corruption.

Holograph. British Museum. Amongst the Newcastle Papers presented by the Earl of Chichester in 1886. *See facsimile on p.* 153.

'I am sorry, my L^d, that y^r illness and other accidents should stopp Hunter's journey. I wish you would dispatch him as soon as you find it possible. Great inconveniences may be occasion'd by his absence. If you will send me the ten thousand £. by West, I shall be glad to receive them to morrow morning, between 10 and 11.

'GEORGE R.'

George II's queen, Caroline Wilhelmina of Anspach, was a marked contrast to her husband. Cultured, witty, and fascinating, her death, in 1737, was a real loss to the English people and to the king. A story, told in a contemporary letter, of her fondness for making a witty speech is worthy of relation. During her last illness, when her physician, who was seeking a divorce from his wife, came to bleed her, she bade him raise his head towards her before he began, saying, 'Let me have a look at your comical face!' and as he commenced the bleeding, added, 'What would you give now that you were cutting your wife?' The signature below is appended to a letter written by her in 1732[1].

Caroline

Just as George II hated his father, Frederick Prince of Wales, as he grew up, hated George II and his chief minister, Walpole. Frederick had come to England much earlier in life than had his father or grandfather, was more conversant with the language and the people, and possessed more English personal friends; amongst them some of the bitterest political foes of Walpole. But for his mother, the Prince seems to have entertained a lively regard. Contemporary letters speak of the affectionate relations existing between them, and of their constant meetings whilst the king was away on the Continent. When, however, George II was in England all this was changed; at the Court balls the prince had his own room, danced with those of his own set, and entertained them at a separate table. In 1737, only a little before the death of the queen, the rupture between the prince and his father became so open that the latter was forced to retire altogether from the Court. In May, 1736, Frederick married the Princess Augusta of Saxe-Gotha. Lady Strafford gives her husband the following account of the lady and of the wedding, which, we see, took place in the evening: 'The Princess is neither handsom nor ugly, tall nor short, but has

---

[1] British Museum. Additional MSS. 32,684, fol. 1.

LETTER FROM GEORGE II TO THE DUKE OF NEWCASTLE.

I am sorry, my Ld that yr illness and other accidents should stopp Hunter's journey. I wish you would dispatch him as soon as you find it possible. Great inconveniency may be occasion'd by his absence. If you will send me the Ten thausend lt. by West, I shall be glad to receive them to morrow morning, between 10. and 11.

George R

XXIII. George the Second and Wilhelmina Carolina, his Wife

a lively pritty countenance enough. The Duke of Grafton told me we ware to meet in the Great Drawing-room, and the Peers and Peeresses to either goe down into the chaple after the Queen, or sitt, during the cerrimony, above in the King's closset (which he said, as a friend, he thought wou'd be the best place). Then We were to see them supp, and then see them abed.' The prince's home was now at Leicester House: here George III was born in

P.S. This was writt half an Hour before the P\[rince]ss was brought to bed of the finest Boy She has had yet. God bless You both, and recover L\[or]d Scarborough soon. I trust You'll not let him come back D\[ea]r Madam till he is thoroughly well. I hope You'll think me in earnest w\[hen] I tell You, You have both no better friend, than,

Frederick P.

1738; and here, with the 'patriots,' as Walpole's opponents styled themselves, plenty of uncomplimentary language was spoken about the king and his advisers. Lord Scarborough was one of the nobility who attached himself to the prince's party, though he did not wholly sever himself from the king's, and he and Lady Scarborough—to whom the letter, the postscript to which appears in the facsimile given above, is addressed—

156   *Handwriting of the Kings and Queens of England*

seem to have been frequent visitors at Leicester House. The boy here referred to was christened Henry Frederick, and became Duke of Cumberland.

In the facsimiles below we have the signature of Frederick's wife, the Princess Augusta; and following that, specimens of the handwriting of other children of George II.

*Believe me allways Dr Madam
Your very affectionate
Augusta*

AUGUSTA, wife of FREDERICK, PRINCE OF WALES.

*I remain your very affectionate friend
William*

WILLIAM AUGUSTUS, DUKE OF CUMBERLAND: born 1721; died, unmarried, 1765.

*St James's Jan 31
1728
I was still happy to find dear D. of Portland that you*

PRINCESS ELIZABETH: died, unmarried, 1758.

Anne *Mary* *Louisa*

PRINCESS ANNE: married the Prince of Orange; died, 1759.

PRINCESS MARY: married the Landgrave of Hesse Cassel; died in 1771.

PRINCESS LOUISA: married Frederick V, King of Denmark; died, 1751.

LETTER WRITTEN BY GEORGE III TO HIS GRANDFATHER WHEN ELEVEN YEARS OF AGE.

I hope You will forgive the Liberty I take to thank Your Majesty for the Honour You did me Yesterday. It is my utmost Wish, and shall allways be my Study to deserve Your Paternal Goodness and Protection. I am with the Greatest Respect and Submission

Sir

Cliffden
June the 23
1749

Your Majestys
Most Humble and most
Dutyfull Subject Grand-Son and Servant

George

XXIV

GEORGE III AND QUEEN CHARLOTTE

GEORGE III has left us some specimens of his handwriting penned at a very early age. The following was written when he was just eleven years old, the period when his mother, regarding with annoyance the influence which the ministers of the country had with her father-in-law, was for ever reminding him 'to be king,' in deed and not only in word, when he ascended the throne.

Holograph. Original at the British Museum. Additional MSS. 32,684, folio 78. Facsimile opposite.

'I hope You will forgive the Liberty I take to thank Your Majesty, for the Honour You did me Yesterday. It is my utmost Wish, and shall allways be my Study, to deserve Your Paternal Goodness and Protection. I am with the Greatest Respect and Submission

'Clifden
'June the 23^d
'1749.

'Sir
'Your Majesty's
'Most Humble and most
'Dutyfull Subject Grand-son and Servant
'GEORGE.'

The favour alluded to was probably a visit, or some mark of attention, which the grandfather was fond of paying to his grandson, though he kept aloof from the boy's father.

160   *Handwriting of the Kings and Queens of England*

His writing seven years later, is shown below in the conclusion of another letter to his grandfather [1].

Kew July the 12th. 1756.

> *Sir*
> *Your Majesty's*
> *Most Dutifull*
> *Grandson, Subject, and Humble Servant.*
> *George P.*

The death of George II, in 1760, put upon the throne of England, the first king of the Hanoverian line who could boast of English birth and bringing-up. The following paragraph in his first speech to Parliament, written with his own hand, shows that George III was himself proud of this circumstance :—

Original at the British Museum, amongst the Newcastle Papers.

> *✠ Born & Educated in this Country I glory in the Name of Britain; & the peculiar happiness of my Life, will ever consist, in promoting the Welfare of a people, whose Loyalty & warm affection to me, I consider, as the greatest & most permanent Security of my Throne.*

'Born and Educated in this Country I glory in the Name of Britain; & the peculiar happiness of my Life, will ever consist, in promoting the Welfare of a people, whose Loyalty & warm affection to me, I consider, as the greatest & most permanent Security of my Throne.'

[1] British Museum. Additional MSS. 32,684, fol. 93

L

HANDWRITING OF CHILDREN OF GEORGE III.

Yours most sincerely

FREDERICK, DUKE OF YORK: born 1763; died 1827; married the Princess Frederica of Prussia.

Ernest

ERNEST, DUKE OF CUMBERLAND AND KING OF HANOVER: born, 1771; died, 1851; married Frederica of Mecklenburg-Strelitz.

Frederick

My dear Nephy
Your truly sincere friend
Adolphus Frederick

ADOLPHUS FREDERICK, DUKE OF CAMBRIDGE: born, 1774; died, 1850; married Augusta of Hesse-Cassel; *father of the present Duke of Cambridge.*

The Princess Charlotte

PRINCESS CHARLOTTE: born, 1766; died, 1828; married the King of Wurtemberg.

Amalie

PRINCESS AMELIA: born, 1783; died, unmarried, 1810.

Augusta Sophia

PRINCESS AUGUSTA SOPHIA: born, 1768; died, unmarried, 1840.

March 25 1812

PRINCESS ELIZABETH: born, 1770; died, 1840; married the Landgrave of Hesse-Homburg.

Windsor Mary
1810

PRINCESS MARY: born, 1776; died, 1840; married her cousin, the Duke of Gloucester.

XXIV. George the Third and Queen Charlotte

The last attack of insanity with which the king was afflicted, demonstrated itself in the early spring of 1810. His handwriting at this date—an example is given below—attached to royal warrants and documents of a similar nature, presents evidence of his complete mental incapacity before he ceased discharging public duties.

He never regained his powers, though he lingered on for ten years, his condition being for the greater part of that time truly pitiable. Queen Charlotte, whom he had married during the year following his accession, died in 1818. As it is said that she captivated George III by a letter which, as a girl, she addressed to the King of Prussia, begging him to spare her country—Mecklenburg-Strelitz—this example of her signature,

appended to a letter addressed to the Earl of Effingham, treasurer of her household, may be of interest[1].

On the opposite page are examples of the handwriting of some of the king's numerous children.

[1] British Museum. Additional MSS. 27,543, fol. 16.

XXV

GEORGE IV, QUEEN CAROLINE, AND THE PRINCESS CHARLOTTE

GEORGE IV was born about a year after his parents' marriage. Both he and his brother Frederick, born in 1763, were, in 1771, placed under the governorship of Lord Holderness, who, after holding this appointment for five years, seems to have been glad to resign it. The reports he sent from time to time to George III revealed the difficulties of his situation, not, it should be said in fairness to the boys, wholly owing to their troublesomeness, but quite as much to the want of unanimity existing amongst the teachers as to the best course of study to be adopted. Still, despite these disadvantages, the boys—especially the Prince of Wales—picked up a good deal of knowledge, though they had little application. How much of the translation of Letter XVII in the Fourth Book of Cicero—which was sent home for the king's perusal when George was about fifteen—is the boy's own work, and how much it was 'touched up' by his tutors, we shall never know, but the facsimile given opposite of the first page of the MS.[1] shows that the prince wrote a good plain hand.

As he grew up, the prince showed signs of an inclination to embrace and follow a moral code very different from that of his father; hence the quarrel between the king for the time being and the Prince of Wales for the time being, which the English people must have taken as a matter of course, since they had witnessed a similar disagreement, though not for the same cause as this, between the sovereign and his eldest son ever since the House of Hanover had come to reign over them.

[1] British Museum. Additional MSS. 20,023.

XXV. George the Fourth, Queen Caroline, Princess Charlotte

George III's ministers showed the prince every mark of disapprobation of his conduct; and it was with some reluctance that the Regency Bill,

TRANSLATION FROM CICERO, BY GEORGE IV WHEN FIFTEEN YEARS OF AGE.

As soon as I heard, your Daughter (Tullia) was dead, I confess I was extremely concerned, as it became me to be, at a loss which I regarded as common to us both; & if I had been with you, I should not have been wanting to you, but should have openly testified the bitterness of my grief. 'Tis true this is but a poor and miserable consolation: because those who ought to administer it, I mean

after the commencement of the king's last illness, in 1810, was agreed to. His signature as Prince Regent appears on the following page[1].

We also give, on the same page, his signature as king attached to the coronation oath. How far he kept that oath towards his country is a matter unnecessary to discuss here.

[1] Original on Royal Warrant. Public Record Office.

To turn the Prince of Wales from the course of life he was following, George III and his ministers were for ever urging him to contract a royal union, but the prince as often rejected all proposals of the kind, till

SIGNATURE OF GEORGE IV AS PRINCE REGENT.

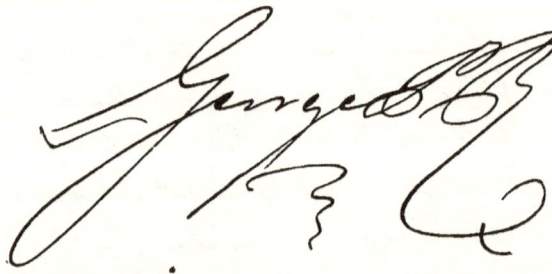

at length, driven almost to distraction by the state of his finances, he yielded to the tempting offer made by the king of a liquidation of his debts, and an increased income, if he would marry his cousin, the Princess Caroline of Brunswick. The marriage, we know, turned out as might

SIGNATURE OF GEORGE IV AS ATTACHED TO THE CORONATION OATH.

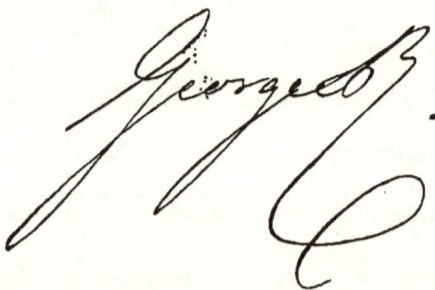

have been expected, though perhaps the lengths to which the prince carried the indignities which he heaped upon his wife, may have astonished even those most nearly acquainted with him. There is no need to recall the incidents of this treatment, which culminated in George IV's refusal to allow the queen 'to take part in, or even be present at, the ceremony

XXV. George the Fourth, Queen Caroline, Princess Charlotte 167

of his coronation at Westminster, July 19, 1821. The accompanying letter was evidently written on her return from the Abbey, from the doors of which she had been actually forced back.

Holograph. Draft. Original at British Museum. Additional MSS. 24,182. folio 17.

'The Queen Requests that his Majesty would be pleased to give an early answer to the Demande which the Queen has made to the Arche-Bishop of Canterbury to be Crowned the following week. Not wishing to increese any new Expense upon the Nation the Queen must trust that after the Publik insult her Majesty has Received to day, the King will grant her just Rights to be crowned as next Monday, and that his Majesty will command the Arche-Bishop of Cantibury to fulfill the Queen's particular desire to confer uppon her that Sacred and August Ceremony.

'The Queen also communicates to His Majesty that during the King's absence in Irreland Her Majesty intends visiting Edinburgh.'

The queen's request was refused, and under this last mortification she rapidly sank, dying on August 7 following. The chief comfort of her life was her only child, the Princess Charlotte, who was born in 1796. The princess's learning and charity are matters that need no enlargement upon here. In May, 1816, she became the wife of the late King Leopold of Belgium, and died in child-bed the following year. Below is an example of her handwriting—the conclusion of a letter, written in 1813, to her friend Mrs. Wightman[1].

[1] Original at the British Museum. Additional MSS. 22,723, fol. 26d.

Admiralty.
Jany 29th 1827.
Late at Night.

Madam.

In answer to Your Ladyship's letter of 15th May I have to remark I cannot forget the many happy hours I spent at Merton with Your Ladyship and must ever feel ourselves for any relation of the late Admiral Lord Nelson. At present I cannot promote Commander Blank by, but shall have in error pleasure in bringing forward this meritorious query officer the instant I can with propriety and ever remain.

J. Rashleigh.

XXVI

WILLIAM IV AND QUEEN ADELAIDE

THE new prospect which, on the unhappy death of the Princ[ess] Charlotte, was opened to the Duke of Clarence gave him very lit[tle] real satisfaction. He had for some time lived the life of an Engli[sh] gentleman at Bushey, where he could meditate over a splendid record [of] naval service, and he did not care for the thought of being King of Engla[nd]. The friends he liked best, and kept up with, were naval friends; so, [no] doubt, on his appointment as Lord High Admiral, he had plenty [of] applications for naval preferment, like that which, we see by the followi[ng] answer, had been made to him by Nelson's widow.

Holograph. Original at the British Museum. Additional MSS. 28,3; folio 7. Facsimile opposite.

                        'Admiralty
                        'June 9th 1827
                        'Late at Night.

'Madam,

    'In answer to Your Ladyship's letter of 15th May, I have to rema[rk] I cannot forget the many happy hours I spent at Paris with Your Ladysh[ip] and must ever feel anxious for any relation of the late Admiral Lord Nels[on]. At present I cannot promote Commander Blankley, but shall have since [the] pleasure in bringing forward this meritorious young officer, the instant [I] can with propriety and ever remain,

                    'Madam,
                    'Yours most truly,
                        'WILLIAM.'

His signature as king appears below [1].

William's altered prospects necessitated a separation from 'Mrs. Jordan' —Dorothy Bland, the actress, with whom he lived so long—and a marriage was, with little delay, arranged and celebrated with the Princess Adelaide, daughter of the Duke of Saxe-Meiningen, who thus became Queen Adelaide. Her usual form of signature appears below. She died in 1849.

[1] From Coronation Roll.

Windsor Castle.
June 22. 1889.

I am anxious
to express to all the
Wardens of Great
Britain & of Ireland
— how deeply truly
& I gratefully I
value & of their
every kindness & great
trouble [illegible]

I thank them all
most warmly for
it & shall value
their gift of the Statue
of King Alfred
of Winchester very
highly — as nothing
I understand can
be more interesting to
honour the places
many & of the nearest
loyalty & affection.

Victoria R. I.

XXVII

VICTORIA

THE signature given in facsimile below is probably the earliest specimen of the handwriting of her present Majesty the Queen. It was penned

when she was but four years old. Her first signature as Queen is taken from the original appended to the coronation oath.

As an example of her Majesty's writing at the present time, it would be impossible to find a more suitable and interesting example than the letter in which she expresses her gratitude to the 'Women of Great Britain and Ireland' for their loyal offering on the occasion of her Jubilee. A facsimile of this letter is given opposite.

176 *Handwriting of the Kings and Queens of England*

The signatures of the Prince Consort and of the Duke and Duchess of Kent, the Queen's father and mother, are here given.

Albert

Edward   *The Duchess of Kent*

EDWARD, DUKE OF KENT, fourth son of
George III; born, 1767; died, 1820;
married Victoria of Saxe-Coburg-Saalfeld.

THE DUCHESS OF KENT
his wife.

Below, we give the signatures of the Prince and Princess of Wales, of their two sons, and also of the Queen's three sons—the Duke of Edinburgh, the Duke of Connaught, and the late Duke of Albany.

Albert Edward P.   *Alexandra*

Albert Victor   *George*

Alfred   *Arthur*

Leopold

THE END

www.ingramcontent.com/pod-product-compliance
Lightning Source LLC
Chambersburg PA
CBHW020249170426

43202CB00008B/287